SUSTAINABLE LIVING
GOING GREEN TO PROTECT THE PLANET

By Juliana Burkhart

Portions of this book originally appeared in *Going Green* by Anne Wallace Sharp.

D1469282

LUCENT
PRESS

Published in 2020 by
Lucent Press, an Imprint of Greenhaven Publishing, LLC
353 3rd Avenue
Suite 255
New York, NY 10010

Designer: Andrea Davison-Bartolotta
Editor: Jennifer Lombardo

Cataloging-in-Publication Data

Names: Burkhart, Juliana.
Title: Sustainable living: going green to protect the planet / Juliana Burkhart.
Description: New York : Lucent Press, 2020. | Series: Hot topics | Includes index.
Identifiers: ISBN 9781534568105 (pbk.) | ISBN 9781534568112 (library bound) | ISBN 9781534568129 (ebook)
Subjects: LCSH: Environmentalism–Juvenile literature. | Energy conservation–Juvenile literature. | Sustainable living–Juvenile literature. | Community life–Environmental aspects--Juvenile literature.
Classification: LCC GE195.5 B86 2020 | DDC 333.79–dc23

Printed in China

Some of the images in this book illustrate individuals who are models. The depictions do not imply actual situations or events

CPSIA compliance information: Batch #BW20KL: For further information contact Greenhaven Publishing LLC, New York, New York at 1-844-317-7404.

Please visit our website, www.greenhavenpublishing.com. For a free color catalog of all our high-quality books, call toll free 1-844-317-7404 or fax 1-844-317-7405.

CONTENTS

Adolescence is a time when many people begin to take notice of the world around them. News channels, blogs, and talk radio shows are constantly promoting one view or another; very few are unbiased. Young people also hear conflicting information from parents, friends, teachers, and acquaintances. Often, they will hear only one side of an issue or be given flawed information. People who are trying to support a particular viewpoint may cite inaccurate facts and statistics on their blogs, and news programs present many conflicting views of important issues in our society. In a world where it seems everyone has a platform to share their thoughts, it can be difficult to find unbiased, accurate information about important issues.

It is not only facts that are important. In blog posts, in comments on online videos, and on talk shows, people will share opinions that are not necessarily true or false, but can still have a strong impact. For example, many young people struggle with their body image. Seeing or hearing negative comments about particular body types online can have a huge effect on the way someone views himself or herself and may lead to depression and anxiety. Although it is important not to keep information hidden from young people under the guise of protecting them, it is equally important to offer encouragement on issues that affect their mental health.

The titles in the Hot Topics series provide readers with different viewpoints on important issues in today's society. Many of these issues, such as students' rights, are of immediate concern to young people. This series aims to give readers factual context on these crucial topics in a way that lets them form their own opinions. The facts presented throughout also serve to empower readers to help themselves or support people they know who are struggling with many of the challenges adolescents face today. Although negative viewpoints are not ignored or downplayed, this series allows young people to see that the challenges they face are not insurmountable. As increasing numbers of young adults join public debates, especially regarding their own rights, learning the facts as well as the views of others will help them decide where they stand—and understand what they are fighting for.

Quotes encompassing all viewpoints are presented and cited so readers can trace them back to their original source, verifying for themselves whether the information comes from a reputable place. Additional books and websites are listed, giving readers a starting point from which to continue their own research. Chapter questions encourage discussion, allowing young people to hear and understand their classmates' points of view as they further solidify their own. Full-color photographs and enlightening charts provide a deeper understanding of the topics at hand. All of these features augment the informative text, helping young people understand the world they live in and formulate their own opinions concerning the best way they can improve it.

Protecting the Planet

For thousands of years, humans have relied on fossil fuels to power the things they use every day. Fossil fuels include coal, oil, and natural gas formed from plants and animals that lived hundreds of millions of years ago. They took millions of years to create—and it would take millions of years for today's plants and animals to create new fossil fuels. For this reason, they are considered nonrenewable resources.

Many people believe that the use of nonrenewable resources should be limited as much as possible. This can be done in many ways; for example, turning off lights and appliances that are not in use is one of the simplest things someone can do. However, going green—also known as sustainability because green advocates are working to make sure the earth can continue to comfortably sustain, or support, life of all kinds—involves going beyond simple practices such as this. Some people are implementing new renewable sources of energy, such as solar power, which creates energy from the sun; hydroelectric energy, which is powered by moving water; and wind energy.

Green advocates also focus on conserving water. This can involve taking shorter showers, turning off the water when brushing teeth, and making sure pipes are not leaky. Some people go beyond these measures by putting in systems to catch rainwater and using it instead of tap water.

Sustainability also involves protecting the land and its resources. Advocates of green living suggest that people think about where they build their homes and communities, preserving enough open space to support different ecosystems.

Pollution may kill plants that animals need for survival. As a result, pollution can threaten entire animal species with extinction. Reducing pollution is an important part of green living.

Oil spills such as the one shown here kill plants and animals, and if the oil gets into the water supply, it can threaten human life as well.

Pollution in the Air and Ground

Pollution happens when part of the environment is poisoned or harmed by human activity. Most pollution in the atmosphere is caused when people burn fossil fuels to produce energy. This energy is used to run cars, trains, airplanes, and other vehicles. It is also used to heat, cool, and light homes, businesses, factories, and cities. When fossil fuels burn, they release smoke and invisible gases such as carbon dioxide and nitrogen dioxide. These gases stay in the air, causing pollution.

Air pollution can have a devastating effect on life. It can make people sick. Many people also believe that air pollution is a major factor in global warming. This term describes a worldwide trend that shows the earth is getting warmer. This, in turn, is a major factor in climate change. In some places, such as in Antarctica and on snow-capped mountains, higher temperatures are causing ice to melt. Scientists worry that the melting of the polar ice caps may reduce the habitat of polar bears and other arctic animals, putting them at risk of extinction. Another effect of climate change is more frequent and more severe natural disasters, such as harsh snowstorms.

Annual Frequency of North Atlantic Tropical Storms

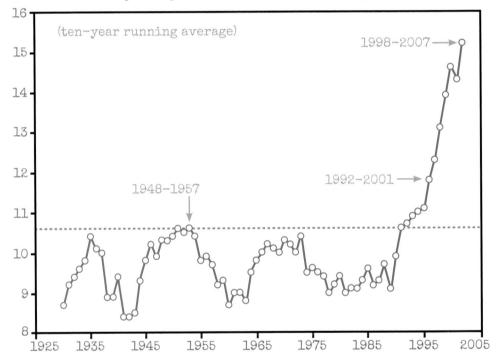

As the temperature of the planet has increased, the number of tropical storms has also increased, as this information from the Pew Research Center shows. Ten-year averages are highlighted with gray arrows.

Pollution of any kind disturbs the ecosystem. Ecosystems are delicate networks that support a variety of life-forms. Any impact on one part of an ecosystem can affect all other parts of it. If people pollute a lake, for instance, the plants and animals that live there may get sick. Some animals might not survive. If one species of plant or animal dies out, the other plants and animals that depend on that species might also die. In the end, the entire food chain may be affected.

Going green means avoiding putting pollution and poisons into the environment. This can be difficult because many poisons have widespread and important uses. Farmers spray their crops with pesticides to kill bugs that eat crops, for instance. Unfortunately, these pesticides are poisonous to other bugs and animals, not just the ones that destroy crops. When farmers spray crops with pesticides, some of the chemicals end up on the ground. When it rains, the rain carries the pesticides into waterways. Gradually, these pesticides may build up in a waterway until they harm the fish or other organisms that live there.

Many people believe it is unhealthy to eat foods sprayed with pesticides or other chemicals. They avoid these foods and choose to eat organic foods, which have not been treated with chemicals. Some people believe organic foods are better for people and the environment. Similarly, green consumers may look for shampoos, soaps, and other health and beauty products made from organic ingredients and wear clothes made only from organic cotton, wool, or silk.

Pesticides are just one of the ways pollution can happen. Many of the paints, glues, and cleaning fluids that are common in homes across America are also toxic, or poisonous, to some forms of life. Many people are going green by trying to rid their homes—and their lives—of these toxins.

Reduce, Reuse, Recycle

People are also concerned about the amount of things people all over the world throw out. The clothes people wear, the newspapers and magazines they read, the toys and electronic games they play—more than three-quarters of this waste is dumped in huge holes in the ground called landfills. When one landfill gets full, another one is opened to hold new garbage. Very few of the things in landfills ever completely break down, or decompose, so they stay there for years.

Many people believe landfills create an environmental hazard. One problem is that some types of waste in landfills ooze into the ground, creating a liquid called leachate. Leachate can cause pollution in surrounding areas. Landfills also sometimes create air pollution; for example, some materials give off a gas called methane, which contributes to global warming, as the garbage decomposes. Other household products found in landfills give off volatile organic compounds (VOCs), which also pollute the air. Landfills also sometimes contain products that have mercury and other toxic chemicals in them, which are released over time as the products break down.

Some environmentalists have targeted landfill waste as a major concern. They separate out materials that can be reused or recycled by grinding them up and making something new out of them. People can also separate food scraps, yard waste, and other biodegradable materials. Biodegradable materials are made of substances that decay relatively quickly, breaking down into elements such as carbon that are recycled naturally. This process is called composting, and compost can be used to fertilize plants.

Green advocates also try to reduce the amount of waste they generate by buying less and using less packaging. They especially try to avoid using nonbiodegradable materials, such as plastic. Nonbiodegradable items never rot, so they will stay in landfills forever.

Everyone has an impact on the earth. It is impossible to completely erase humanity's impact on the environment or reach the ultimate goal of zero waste. However, people can make a difference. Even minor changes to daily habits—such as taking a shorter shower or turning off lights that are not being used—can protect valuable resources. Many people are making more substantial changes to their lives to help protect the environment. They walk or bike where they need to go; they power their homes with solar or wind power; they grow their own organic foods. In many ways, an increasing number of people around the world are recognizing the need to do what they can to preserve and protect the earth and its resources for future generations.

CHAPTER 1

Why Americans Are Going Green

In the beginning of the 19th century, scientists around the world began to notice that the overall temperature on the surface of the earth was rising. They argued that as cities grew larger and relied more on coal for energy to power homes and factories, the warming effect intensified. Carbon dioxide, methane, and ozone gases are produced when fossil fuels such as coal are burned for energy. As these gases build up in the earth's atmosphere, they trap energy from sun, which is reflected back to Earth and warms the surface of the planet. Scientists call these gases greenhouse gases, and the warming they create is sometimes called the greenhouse effect. This is because, in a greenhouse where plants are grown, the glass of the greenhouse reflects heat back into the building and warms the air.

Global warming is often compared to a greenhouse, which traps heat inside so it can stay warm to help plants grow.

The gradual warming of the surface of the planet causes the temperature of the oceans to increase as well. As snow and ice at the earth's north and south poles melt, sea levels around the world are rising. According to a 2014 report from the Intergovernmental Panel on Climate Change (IPCC), "Recent climate changes have had widespread impacts on human and natural systems."[1] As global warming leads to climate change around the world, many plants and animals find it harder to survive or find food as their habitats change. Weather systems have become harder to predict, and the number of devastating floods, hurricanes, and tsunamis has increased around the globe.

Over many millennia, the earth has experienced natural periods of warming and cooling. However, nearly all scientists now agree that the current period of warming is happening much faster and is having much greater effects than any in the past. According to the IPCC, atmospheric concentrations of greenhouse gases have risen to unprecedented levels since the industrial era, and they are now higher than they have been in at least the last 800,000 years. The effects of these gases "have been detected throughout the climate system and are *extremely likely* to have been the dominant cause of the observed warming since the mid-20th century."[2]

Smoke from factories—such as the ones in the center of this picture—contributes to global warming because it contains carbon dioxide. However, not all clouds that come from buildings contain pollutants. The nuclear power plant on the far left is emitting steam, not smoke, so it is not putting greenhouse gases into the atmosphere.

Experts agree that the facts are indisputable: The temperature of the earth is rising faster than ever, and human activities are the primary cause. If societies do not act immediately, scientists predict that global temperatures will continue to rise—with devastating results.

Why Go Green?

"Going green" means different things to different people, but in general, it is the idea that individuals, organizations, and businesses can make an effort to reduce their negative impact on the environment. To some people, that might mean using fewer fossil fuels by switching to a more efficient car or carpooling to work. Some people choose to buy organic groceries and carry their goods home in reusable bags. Others think of going green as furnishing their home with the latest energy-saving devices and appliances.

Bringing reusable bags to the grocery store helps cut down on single-use plastics. This is one choice many people make in an effort to live a more sustainable life.

The History of Earth Day

In the 1960s, there was little concern for environmental issues. Cars ran on gas with the toxic element lead in it, smoke billowed from factory smokestacks, and many companies dumped toxic waste into America's waterways. April 22, 1970–the first Earth Day–marked the beginning of a change.

Earth Day 1970 was partially inspired by the protests Americans were staging to fight for civil rights and to oppose the Vietnam War. Organizers held rallies across America in which an estimated 20 million Americans took part, coming together to demonstrate their commitment to the environment.

Over the past several decades, Earth Day has evolved. The message of Earth Day changes as environmental needs and priorities change, but the goal remains the same: to call attention to environmental issues. Today, as in 1970, people come together each April 22 to celebrate the earth. Educators and environmentalists use Earth Day as a reminder not only of what the earth has to offer, but also of people's responsibility to care for it.

Many people do these things without considering themselves to be "green." They may conserve energy to save money or recycle because their local government requires them to. However, as global concern for climate change increases, more and more people are making a conscious effort to reduce their impact on the environment. There are many ways to go green, and someone's choices might vary based on their lifestyle.

Environmentalism Goes Mainstream

A number of Hollywood actors and actresses have used their fame to lobby on behalf of the environment and bring public attention to the crisis of global warming. Academy Award–winning actor Leonardo DiCaprio has championed environmental issues for many years. Through the Leonardo DiCaprio Foundation, he has spread awareness of environmental issues and produced

PROGRESS IS POSSIBLE

"Solutions to the key environmental challenges are available, achievable and affordable, especially when compared to the expected economic growth and the costs and consequences of inaction."

–Angel Gurría, secretary general of the Organization for Economic Cooperation and Development (OECD)

Quoted in "OECD: Tackle Environmental Problems Now or Pay More Later," ENS-Newswire, March 6, 2008. www.ens-newswire.com/ens/mar2008/2008-03-06-01.html.

several films, including *Global Warning* in 2003 and *Water Planet* in 2005. In 2007, he coproduced, cowrote, and narrated an environmental documentary called *The 11th Hour*, and in 2016, his film *Before the Flood* was released, in which he meets with leaders around the world to discuss climate change.

Perhaps the best-known documentary about the environment is *An Inconvenient Truth*, which hit theaters in 2006. In the film, former vice president Al Gore warns people of the devastating effect that global warming will have if it is unchecked. "The world won't 'end' overnight in ten years," Gore said. "But a point will have been passed, and there will be an irreversible slide into destruction."[3]

An Inconvenient Truth was a surprise hit. It won many awards, including the 2007 Academy Award for Best Documentary Feature. However, more important than the awards to Gore and others involved in making the movie was its impact on the American public. It spurred a new group of people

Actor Leonardo DiCaprio, who is well-known for his roles in movies such as Titanic *and* The Great Gatsby, *has also produced a number of environmental films.*

into action and helped motivate many people to be more environmentally conscious.

Some scientists feel that Gore exaggerated some of the claims in the movie. "I don't want to pick on Al Gore," said Don J. Easterbrook, professor of geology at Western Washington University in Bellingham, Washington. "But there are a lot of inaccuracies in the statements we are seeing, and we have to temper that with real data."[4]

FEWER SALES, HIGHER COST

"There are cost-saving things and specialized labor/machines that reduce production costs. Efficiency improves over time with large numbers. Since green isn't yet mainstream, many of those cost-cutting advantages haven't been adopted by green manufacturers."

—Tony Green, clean technology professional

Tony Green, "Why Going Green Is So Expensive," Speaking Green Communications, April 27, 2017.
www.speakinggreencommunications.com/why-going-green-is-so-expensive/.

Misleading Information

In order to appeal to the growing number of green consumers, more businesses are selling green items. However, some companies exaggerate their "greenness." They may change the name of a product, create packaging that indicates a product is natural, or emphasize a product's organic materials in its advertising or promotional materials. Greenwashing describes the act of misleading consumers about the health or environmental benefits of brands, products, and services. Scot Case, vice president of an environmental marketing firm called TerraChoice, used the example of a shampoo with packaging that promised a "totally organic experience" but included "zero evidence that the product contained any organic ingredients." He added, "We saw absolutely ridiculous claims [from products]. And vague, too. What the heck does 'earth-friendly' mean?"[5]

"Consumers are inundated [flooded] with products that make green claims," added Scott McDougall, the president of

TerraChoice. "Some are accurate, certified and verifiable, while others are just plain fibbing to sell products."[6] In one recent example, Starbucks was accused of greenwashing in 2018 after eliminating most of its plastic straws and using sippy cup-style lids instead. While many people have campaigned to get restaurants to stop giving out plastic straws, which do not biodegrade and frequently end up polluting the ocean, Starbucks's new lids were found to contain more plastic than the old straws did, meaning their change had no real effect on the goal of eliminating sources of single-use plastic.

Federal Agencies

Several government agencies and nonprofit organizations are working to pave the way for the environment. ENERGY STAR, for instance, is a joint program of the U.S. Environmental Protection Agency (EPA) and the U.S. Department of Energy. The purpose of the ENERGY STAR program is to encourage the use of energy-efficient products and practices. Through the program, the federal government labels products in more than 50 product categories, including computer equipment and household appliances. The ENERGY STAR label is used for products that work as well as similar models while using less energy.

Programs such as ENERGY STAR work because people know that energy-efficient appliances are better for the environment and can save them money on their electric bills. Therefore, they generally choose appliances with the ENERGY STAR label over ones that do not have it.

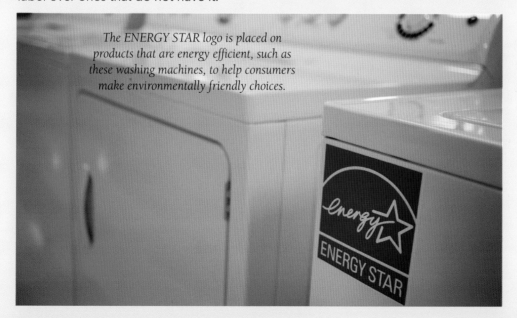

The ENERGY STAR logo is placed on products that are energy efficient, such as these washing machines, to help consumers make environmentally friendly choices.

Many critics accuse the bottled water industry of greenwashing. Many bottled water companies emphasize the "naturalness" of the water, ignoring the fact that the plastic bottle is damaging to the environment. A lot of energy goes into bottling water, and the plastic is nonbiodegradable—it will remain in landfills forever. Of course, no company wants to remind consumers of the damaging effects its products have on the environment.

A discarded plastic water bottle does not decompose.

Some people accuse the entire green movement of being involved in a type of greenwashing. They argue that the costs of going green often outweigh the benefits. The recycling industry offers one example. Large trucks are needed to collect the recyclables, but these trucks burn fossil fuels and pollute the air. Energy is also needed to sort and clean recyclables, a process that sometimes uses a considerable amount of water. Sometimes the detergents used to clean recyclables run off into waterways, polluting the water. Special equipment may be needed to keep harmful waste products from escaping into the air, water, and soil, and further resources are needed to create and power this equipment.

Clearly, going green is not as simple as it appears. It is sometimes difficult to know which choices are best for the

Carbon Offsetting

Carbon offsetting begins with the practice of calculating how much an individual or organization has contributed to carbon emissions through activities such as driving, flying, shipping goods, or using energy. This amount is known as their carbon footprint. People can "erase" their carbon footprint by buying carbon offsets, which fund activities that reduce greenhouse gas emissions. For instance, some programs might pay for wind farms, which produce clean energy to replace fossil fuels, or the planting of forests, which provide trees to help clean the air by absorbing carbon dioxide. When a person buys 10 tons of carbon offsets, for instance, the seller guarantees that 10 fewer tons of pollution go into the atmosphere.

Critics say that some carbon offset programs are better than others, and with so many options to choose from, it is difficult for consumers to know which are best. Others say there is no way of knowing whether carbon offsetting programs really make a difference. *Businessweek* studied six programs that had received funds from carbon offsets. Five of the six said the offsets had not played a significant role in their decision to cut emissions. Offsets went to the utility company in Catawba County, North Carolina, which turned gas from its landfill into electricity. "It's just icing on the cake," said Barry Edwards, director of utilities and engineering in Catawba County. "We would have done this project anyway."[1]

1. Quoted in Ben Elgin, "Another Inconvenient Truth," *Bloomberg Businessweek*, March 26, 2007. www.bloomberg.com/news/articles/2007-03-25/another-inconvenient-truth.

ENERGY SYSTEMS OVERHAUL

"What we need to combat climate change is a complete transformation of our energy system, and that requires a lot of new stuff to be built and installed, some of it in places that are relatively untouched."

—Stephen Tindale, executive director of Greenpeace UK

Quoted in Heather Timmons, "A Renewable Source, and Clean, but Not Without Its Critics," *New York Times*, August 3, 2006, p. C1.

environment. Several programs and organizations have emerged to help with this problem. In addition to ENERGY STAR, which is used primarily for appliances, special certification is given to buildings that meet certain eco-friendly standards. Consumers can also look for green labels on products. EcoLogo and Green Seal are two such examples. Both of these programs look at the entire life cycle of a product, from the materials used to create it to what happens to it when it is disposed of.

With the many claims of companies trying to capture the attention of "green" consumers, it is the responsibility of individuals to learn and understand which programs and products are best for the environment.

Traveling Green

Cars have a place in American culture that is unique compared to most other countries. Because the United States is so large and public transportation is lacking in many areas, cars have come to be seen as a representation of freedom, allowing people to travel wherever they want in a relatively short amount of time. For this reason, a car is seen as an essential possession for the majority of Americans. However, as evidence of cars' negative impact on the environment has become more apparent, many Americans have started to trade driving their cars for walking or biking on their daily commutes. As a woman named Tanya Mead explained,

> Anyone who knows me knows that I love to walk nearly everywhere I go … My local grocery store is about two miles away from my home. If there are only a few things that I need, I can easily stroll over there and back. I much prefer this to getting in a car and zipping over. Of course, the car method is more practical if I have a full week's worth of groceries to buy, but if it's just a handful of items, the walk is just fine with me.[7]

Studies show that a vast array of health benefits can be obtained from exercise, but the impact on the environment is also significant, especially when large numbers of people give up four-wheeled transport in favor of methods that emit fewer greenhouse gases.

Human-Powered Transportation

The most obvious way to go green is to get out of the car. According to the U.S. Department of Transportation, American adults drive 15 million miles every day for trips that are only a half mile or less—a distance it would take the average person just 10 minutes to walk. All this driving burns valuable fossil fuels and contributes to air pollution.

Biking to work or school is one way people can reduce their impact on the environment.

In addition to helping the environment, walking is part of a healthier lifestyle. One woman named Lois Fletcher lost 30 pounds (13.6 kg) when she stopped using her car and began riding the transit system in Atlanta, Georgia, instead. She walked four or five miles per day, including up and down the stairs. "In my old office, the parking garage was right there," she said. "I could park 30 feet from my desk. I have diabetes and high blood pressure, and my doctor would say if you would just walk for 30 minutes, that would really help, but I could never find the time to do it. With three boys, when I got off work, the last thing I thought about was exercise."[8]

Biking is also gaining popularity as a green mode of transportation. To appeal to the growing number of people who bike daily to school, to work, or on errands, bike manufacturers are increasingly producing lightweight bikes that are easy to store. Some bicycles have extra, helpful items such as a headlight that is powered by pedaling, a rack for carrying a briefcase or other essentials, or a cup holder for coffee or a bottle of water. Some bikers are fitting their bikes with electric motors that supply more power when needed. Electric bikes enable people to go farther and navigate hilly roads with less effort. In May 2019, the website Tech Crunch reported that investors backed a company called Bond Mobility that is developing an electric bike that can go up to 30 miles (48 km) per hour. The company hopes to make the bike available for city dwellers as an alternative to cars. This would reduce traffic, make it easier for people to find parking spots, and eliminate thousands of pounds of carbon emissions. In the future, this type of bike might be a common sight in big cities around the world.

A study from the Institute for Transportation and Development Policy (ITDP) calculated that carbon emissions from urban transportation could be 11 percent lower if cities could get 14 percent of their urban travelers to convert to bicycling by the year 2050. As of 2019, the ITDP estimates that 6 percent of urban travel is already done by bike, but that more than half of those bicycling miles come from a small number of countries. If larger countries such as the United States could get more commuters to travel by bike, the impact would be much

The Evolution of the Hybrid

At the 1995 Tokyo Auto Show, Toyota demonstrated a futuristic hybrid concept vehicle, which consisted of an electric motor connected to a regular gasoline engine. Toyota called its car the Prius. By 2000, Toyota was selling the Prius in more than 90 markets worldwide. As other hybrid vehicles became available to consumers, Toyota expanded its Prius line to include larger models with more space for families. By January 2017, the Prius liftback model was the world's top selling hybrid vehicle, with more than 4 million cars sold worldwide.

Although hybrid cars can be very helpful to the environment, they do have some drawbacks. For instance, concerns have been raised about what will happen to the car's lithium-ion battery when it can no longer be recharged and must be replaced. Lithium-ion batteries can be recycled, but many people do not bother to take the steps to do so; according to the *Guardian*, only about 5 percent of batteries in the European Union (EU) are currently recycled. This can be harmful to the environment. Furthermore, mining for the materials needed to create batteries has destroyed certain areas—often in impoverished or conflicted regions where the local residents do not benefit from or are actively harmed by the mining and have little or no say in whether it takes place. To address these issues, many people are working on developing alternative ways to power hybrid cars.

The Toyota Prius was one of the first hybrid vehicles available to American consumers.

greater. However, not everyone believes replacing cars with bikes—especially ones that can go so fast—is a good idea. Some commuters worry that biking during rush hour is too dangerous. People are more likely to consider biking to work and school if their city offers safer conditions, such as bike lanes.

Bike lanes make bicycle travel safer, especially in big cities.

Public Transport

Walking or biking might not be practical for longer trips. Some people ride buses, subways, or trains to get where they need to go. The more people ride together, the less fuel and less air pollution there is per person. William W. Millar, former president of the American Public Transportation Association (APTA), agreed, saying, "Riding public transportation is one of the most powerful weapons Americans have in combating global climate change."[9]

However, many communities are not well served by public transportation, so it is not a practical option for everyone. Even in some places where people can take the bus or train, it is inconvenient. Some people also think the fares are too high. As a result, fewer than 5 percent of Americans routinely use mass transit systems to get to and from work. Even fewer use it for shopping, errands, or visiting friends.

Where public transportation is unavailable or inconvenient, people sometimes carpool to school or work, joining with others who are headed their way. In some places, private businesses have helped encourage carpooling by providing message boards or other networks for people to find potential riders or drivers who live in their area. Vanpooling has emerged as another option: Some companies buy vans that can be used the same way a school bus is—picking up all the employees in an area and taking them directly to work.

In 2006, Wyeth Pharmaceuticals, a large drug manufacturer, was recognized by the EPA for its efforts to reduce its impact on the environment. The company's Commuter Assistance Center coordinated transportation and commuter programs for more than 13,000 employees at its various work sites. The center matched employees by residence, work hours, and office location for carpool and vanpool groups, and a free shuttle service for employees transported mass transit riders from public transportation centers to work. Each month, participants in the program saved almost 1 million miles of driving and close to 40,000 gallons of fuel.

Another strategy many people use is to combine trips. Rather than taking several trips and returning home after each one, green consumers run all their errands on the same day and work out an efficient path that will reduce the amount of time they spend driving. This is an easy way for people to cut back on the number of miles they drive and reduce their carbon dioxide emissions.

Clean Energy

Driving less is not the only way to reduce pollution. Drivers can also choose cleaner fuels for their cars. Biofuels, for example, are made from plants. Ethanol is the most common biofuel. It is generally made from corn, but it can also be made from other plants, including wheat, sugar, and sorghum. Ethanol is typically mixed with gasoline because this makes it more efficient; a mix of ethanol and gasoline allows a car to get more miles per gallon than pure ethanol would. E85—a combination of 85 percent ethanol and 15 percent conventional gasoline—is generally less expensive than gasoline, delivers slightly more horsepower, and gets only slightly lower fuel mileage. Experts say that powering a car with E85 reduces greenhouse gas emissions by as much as 70 percent.

Biodiesel is another biofuel. Biodiesel is made from refined vegetable oils such as soy, canola, and recycled restaurant grease. Biodiesel can be used in any car or truck with a diesel engine. Generally, 20 percent biodiesel is mixed with 80 percent diesel—a formula called B20. B20 reduces carbon emissions by about 30 percent. Commercial biodiesel may be more expensive than regular diesel or gasoline, but the fuel economy is significantly better. Like other biofuels, it is biodegradable. According to the OECD and the International Energy Agency, the United States aims to have 12 percent of the energy it uses for transportation come from biofuel by the year 2025.

Restaurant grease can be turned into fuel. This is good for two reasons: The grease does not pollute the environment and people have the option to cut down on their use of fossil fuels.

A SLOW PROCESS

"Electric cars are not going to take the market by storm, but it's going to be a gradual improvement."

—Carlos Ghosn, chairman and chief executive officer of the Renault-Nissan-Mitsubishi Alliance

Quoted in Dave Lee, "Nissan-Renault Head Carlos Ghosn's Zero Emission Goal," BBC, February 9, 2010. news.bbc.co.uk/2/hi/business/8501348.stm.

Another fuel alternative is propane, which is frequently used for gas grills and camping stoves. In March 2008, the Yellow Cab Company in Las Vegas, Nevada, announced that it was converting some of the cars in its fleet to run on both gasoline and propane. "Propane burns more cleanly than gasoline," explained a Yellow Cab spokesperson. "The converted propane cabs are said to run 15 to 20 mpg [miles per gallon] farther than non-converted cabs with one-half the [carbon dioxide] emissions."[10] In the following years, Yellow Cab cars in other cities, including Pittsburgh, Pennsylvania, and Columbus, Ohio, also switched over to some propane-fueled cars.

Many communities are also trying to reduce the carbon footprint of city streetcars, trains, and buses. Some have converted their fleets to run on natural gas, which burns more cleanly than other fossil fuels. Others are using biofuels. For example, in 2008, the city bus company in St. Cloud, Minnesota, introduced a bus powered by recycled deep-fryer vegetable oil. The light rail line in Minneapolis, Minnesota, uses wind energy to power its trains.

One of the main disadvantages of these newer fuels is that, because they are not in widespread use, they are sometimes hard to find. One driver of a car that runs on compressed natural gas (CNG) explained,

> For most people, it isn't really a big deal if you start running low on fuel in your gasoline-powered car. Unless you're in a few remote places, a gas station is likely only a few short miles away. That's not the case with our Civic GX ... The nearest CNG fueling stations are either at a public utility ... about 25 miles away [from home] or in the industrial outskirts ... (30 miles).[11]

Problems with Using Food as Fuel

Some people worry that growing corn and other crops for fuel is taking land that should be used to provide food to the planet's growing population. The Food and Agriculture Organization (FAO) of the United Nations estimates that by the year 2050, the world will need to produce 70 percent more calories' worth of food to keep up with the growing global population. According to the FAO, of all the habitable land on Earth, 50 percent is already being used for agriculture. Of that 50 percent, 77 percent is used for livestock and feed, yet meat and dairy account for only 17 percent of the world's calorie supply. This data raises interesting questions about how societies can effectively use their limited farmland to produce enough food to feed everyone in the world.

Hybrid and Electric Cars

For people who need or want a car, hybrids are an attractive choice. Hybrid cars run on gasoline at high speeds but switch to battery power at low speeds or when stopped—at a red light, for instance. This offers a more fuel-efficient and cleaner option. According to some experts, hybrids get much better gas mileage than traditional cars. The Toyota Prius, for instance, gets an estimated 54 miles (87 km) per gallon in the city. Even the smallest cars running on gas generally do not get more than 30 miles (48 km) per gallon.

Today's hybrids cost between $3,000 and $4,000 more than traditional cars, but many people are willing to spend the money because they believe the gas savings will make them less expensive in the long run. Elizabeth Rogers and Thomas M. Kostigen, the authors of *The Green Book: The Everyday Guide to Saving the Planet One Simple Step at a Time*, estimated that the average driver of a hybrid saves more than 20 gallons of gasoline a month. "If an additional 1 percent of vehicles sold in the United States per year were hybrids, the gasoline saved would fill nearly 4,600 tanker trucks,"[12] Rogers and Kostigen stated. Hybrids are particularly fuel efficient in cities because city driving involves frequent stops at red lights and in slow traffic, so the car switches over to battery power often.

GREEN GOES MAINSTREAM

"The green, sustainability movement is going mainstream ... we want to ride that wave."

—Steve Case, founder of AOL and investor in alternative vehicle projects

Quoted in Annys Shin, "Internet Visionaries Betting on Green Technology Boom," *Washington Post*, April 18, 2006, www.washingtonpost.com/archive/business/2006/04/18/internet-visionaries-betting-on-green-technology-boom-span-classbankheadvast-market-huge-profit-potential-beckon-investorsspan/e7d03c10-40e0-40a2-b33f-f9805a22b072/.

Not everyone is convinced that hybrids are the sustainable solution of the future, however. The Toyota Prius, the first hybrid, gets a 50 percent efficiency boost from its hybrid technology, but other hybrids get just 10 percent or less. In fact, the Union of Concerned Scientists says that half of all hybrid vehicles currently on the market are no more fuel efficient than their nonhybrid versions.

Another option for a nontraditional car is an electric car. As the name implies, electric vehicles are powered by electricity; they do not use gasoline at all. Generally, the vehicles are equipped with battery packs that can be recharged by simply plugging the car into a wall socket or special charging station.

Electric vehicles generate 60 percent fewer greenhouse gas emissions than gasoline-powered vehicles, and they cost less to operate. Steve Heckeroth of the American Solar Energy Society stated that electric cars cost roughly 2 cents per mile, compared to at least 20 to 30 cents per mile for vehicles fueled by gasoline, ethanol, or biodiesel.

In 2008, the American automotive company Tesla started building the first electric cars for consumers. However, with a high price point and low range of mileage before the vehicles needed to be recharged, most consumers found them to be too impractical. By 2018, Tesla had re-engineered its cars to get better mileage, making them more popular with drivers. Today,

Shown here is a Tesla car at a charging station.

Tesla is the world's best-selling electric car. Vehicles can only be purchased online or at company-owned showrooms; this allows Tesla to avoid having to navigate conventional car dealerships and enables buyers to customize their cars, resulting in lower price points. By 2017, there were more than 3 million electric cars on the world's roads.

Hydrogen Fuel Cells

Hydrogen fuel cell vehicles use hydrogen gas to power their electric motors, producing nothing except heat and water vapor as byproducts. These vehicles are only just beginning to enter the U.S. market, and hydrogen refueling stations are not widely available; however, many states are taking initiatives to build hydrogen refueling stations where drivers can purchase pressurized hydrogen and fill their vehicle in just 10 minutes. Just as plug-in electric cars were once impractical but are now widely used, experts predict that hydrogen fuel cell vehicles will become more accessible to everyone as technology improves.

While hydrogen-powered cars do have many benefits, they are not without their drawbacks. For starters, while hydrogen can be easily obtained from water by separating hydrogen from oxygen, this requires energy, either from fossil fuels or renewable sources. Thus, hydrogen is only as emission-free as the energy that is used to obtain it. Another obstacle to hydrogen gas is that it must be compressed or liquefied in order to fit into the size of a typical car's gasoline tank. Currently, this is expensive to do, so hydrogen fuel is not widely available.

In 2017, Hyundai took this hydrogen-powered car on tour to raise awareness for alternative energy vehicles.

EXAGGERATING GREEN CLAIMS

"The environmental rhetoric coming out of the last two years of 'eco' auto shows does not reflect true vehicle production. The industry's goal has been to fool consumers into believing that automakers are producing eco-conscious cars. Nothing could be further from the truth."

—Jodie Van Horn, spokesperson for Rainforest Action Network

Quoted in "Shades of Green at the North American International Auto Show," Environmental News Service, January 16, 2008. www.ens-newswire.com/ens/jan2008/2008-01-16-03.html.

Travel by Air

Although technology for green vehicles has come a long way since the early 2010s, there is still a lot of progress to be made when it comes to air travel. In her 2008 book *Gorgeously Green*, Sophie Uliano called flying "an environmental nightmare."[13] According to Dan Imhoff, author of *Paper or Plastic*, an airplane's takeoff uses the same amount of energy as 2.4 million lawnmowers running for 20 minutes. Uliano added that flying is much worse than driving "because the toxic chemicals that are spewed out are much closer to the ozone layer—they go straight in, whereas on the ground, many of them evaporate on their way up."[14]

No matter how much people love the environment, they might be unable to simply give up flying altogether. Many Americans live on one coast and have family on another. Others have jobs that take them to other places in the country and around world. An increasing number of Americans who are concerned about the environmental costs of flying are buying carbon offsets to make up for the polluting effects of flying.

However, some people believe this is not enough to address the environmental problems flying causes. Joe Romm, an expert who has testified before Congress on carbon offsets, believes that carbon offsetting gives people the idea that all they have to do is plant a few trees to make up for air pollution when they fly. "It's very unproductive to leave people with the impression that we could possibly plant our way out of the problem,"[15] he said.

Scientists at Boeing, the National Aeronautics and Space Administration (NASA), and other organizations are looking for ways to make airplanes greener. In the meantime, many Americans are planning to cut back their air travel. For example, some people choose to spend their vacations closer to home so they do not need to take a plane at all. However, experts say that finding more eco-friendly forms of jet fuel is a better long-term solution than requiring people to drastically change their travel habits. Research is ongoing in this area.

CHAPTER 3

Greener Homes

When Michael Reynolds graduated from architecture school in 1969, he was not interested in designing buildings made out of wood and bricks. Instead, he wanted to develop inexpensive building materials that could be made out of recycled items. He began to experiment with garbage such as glass bottles, empty tin cans, and old tires pounded full of dirt. He reasoned that by using these materials in buildings, he could both remove trash from landfills and develop structures that used less energy. He called these structures Earthships. Earthships are built from natural and repurposed materials, and they heat and cool themselves without using fossil fuels. They use solar and wind energy, and they also collect rainwater to be used for drinking, cooking, and doing laundry within the home. Earthships generally contain a greenhouse where organic food can be grown to feed the family that lives there. In some cases, these homes run entirely "off the grid," meaning they do not rely on power or water companies.

Today, Earthship Biotecture builds Earthships for people who want to live in them and educates others on the principles of how to build them. According to the company's website, "Tires are the perfect form for a rammed-earth brick. There's no shortage of used tires—at least 2.5 billion are currently stockpiled in the United States, with 2.5 million more discarded every year."[16] Earthship Biotecture also organizes relief projects to serve areas that have experienced natural disasters. For instance, after Hurricane Maria devasted Puerto Rico in 2017, volunteers

Used tires are a cheap and plentiful source of building materials.

traveled to the island to collect trash materials and used them to build housing for people who had lost their homes. Because Earthships are partially built into the earth itself, they are highly resistant to natural disasters such as earthquakes and hurricanes.

Alternative Building Methods

Earthships are beautiful and highly efficient homes. They are becoming more popular around the world, but they are still very rare compared to the conventional homes where most people live. "I believe that buildings are the worst thing that people do to the environment," said Rob Watson, a scientist with the Natural Resources Defense Council (NRDC). "We don't associate the fact that when we turn on a light switch, coal is mined in a mine; it goes to a power plant that comes up the stack as acid rain producing sulfur dioxide, planet-cooking carbon dioxide. There's no direct connection between the environmental impact that the building causes and the damage is always somewhere else."[17] Watson also noted, "Buildings use twice as much energy as cars and trucks. Seventy percent of the electricity in the United States is consumed by our homes and our office buildings."[18]

Architects, developers, builders, homeowners, and others have sought to address these problems through sustainable building. Although the methods sustainable builders use vary considerably—and the resulting buildings vary even more—the goals typically include conservation of natural resources in building materials and ongoing energy requirements, the improvement of indoor air quality, and the reduction of environmental impacts.

So what is green and what is not? To help identify how green a building is, the U.S. Green Building Council created a rating system called the Leadership in Energy and Environmental Design, or LEED. LEED provides guidelines for sustainable building in five key areas: sustainable site development, water savings, energy efficiency, materials selection, and indoor environmental quality. Architects, developers, builders, and others often use LEED standards to help them reduce the impact of their projects on the environment.

Installing solar panels is one way a building can boost its LEED rating.

MAKING IT EASIER TO GO GREEN

"Green design is getting easier, but doing the right thing shouldn't be so darn hard ... Industries should be required to do the research and to provide unbiased information, so architects can select products that work from the traditional standpoint of beauty, cost, and durability, and just compare environmental impact numbers across products. We need to keep encouraging the building industry to be more responsible so we don't have to be so smart."

—Jason McLennan, architect and author of several books on architecture and sustainable design

Quoted in Cheryl Weber, "Green Design Gets Practical," *Architect*, March 16, 2005. www.architectmagazine.com/technology/green-design-gets-practical_o.

The National Association of Home Builders (NAHB), a trade association representing home builders and remodelers, has also created the NAHB Sustainability Toolkit. The toolkit program includes educational videos and online courses for builders and buyers, reports on national green building programs, and sustainability checklists to assess projects for their environmental impact.

Private homes and businesses are not the only ones going green. Across America, government buildings—including city halls, police stations, courthouses, and public housing developments—are being built according to strict environmental standards. In 2005, Washington became the first state to pass green building legislation. According to the law, all major public buildings, including public schools, are required to meet or exceed LEED standards in construction or renovation.

Green Hotels

To attract the business of eco-friendly consumers, many hotels around the world are adopting measures to go green. For example, Hotel Rural Vale do Rio in Portugal operates on 100 percent renewable energy, including vegetable oil biodiesel, wind, and hydro power. Regulated water taps in each room help control the hotel's use of water. In 2018, the hotel bought Tesla electric cars for use on the grounds. The effects of these initiatives have been far-reaching: Guests have taken note and have shown a greater interest in implementing more sustainability efforts in their travel plans.

Other hotels are taking similar steps and attracting eco-conscious travelers. Many of these green hotels are built with locally sourced materials and are designed to minimize unnecessary energy use. For example, the Six Senses Con Dao resort in Vietnam was built in a way that maximizes airflow so people do not feel like they need to use much air conditioning.

Landscaping and Location

The first step in green building is to consider the entire landscape when deciding where to build. One of the goals of sustainable development, no matter how big the building will be, is to preserve as much of the natural environment as possible. Green developers avoid cutting down trees or filling in wetlands. Some build houses in small groups on one part of the land so the rest can be preserved as trails, parkland, forest, or even a working farm. Prairie Crossing, a famous conservation development with 359 homes in Grayslake, Illinois, includes a large farm that produces organic vegetables, fruit, flowers, and eggs for residents and the surrounding public.

GLOBALLY GREEN

"The key mistake is not taking a global view of what green building is. People focus on health issues, supply chain issues, design issues—but you need to look at all of these things together."

—Steve Thomas, resident at Planet Green, a green educational media resource

Quoted in Matt Woolsey, "Nine Earth-Friendly Fixes for Your Home," *Forbes*, April 14, 2008. www.forbes. com/2008/04/14/green-home-energy-forbeslife-cx_mw_0414realestate.html.

Green developers also plan buildings on sites that take advantage of the landscape. They use the sun, wind, trees, and other plants to provide heating, cooling, lighting, ventilation, and shade. Experts say that in cold climates, positioning a building along the east-west axis, so the long side of the building faces directly south, can save 25 percent on heating bills because this is the side that gets the most sun—and therefore the most heat. In warmer climates, green developers position windows and walls to maximize breezes and use awnings and trees to help shade windows from the sun.

The size of the home also matters. Larger houses have a larger carbon footprint. They take up more land, leaving less room for plants, trees, and animals to live. They use more building materials. They also require more energy to heat, cool, and light. "If you have a family of three it's ridiculous to be in a 5,000-square-foot house because you can't recover the energy resources," said one green builder. "You could put in the greenest everything, but you'll never catch up if the house is too big."[19]

The tiny house movement has been gaining popularity in recent years. These houses are very environmentally friendly, and many can be moved around, making travel easier.

Renewable Materials

A green building starts with materials that have a low impact on the earth. Sustainable building materials are renewable and can be grown organically. For instance, bamboo has become a popular building material. Bamboo is a grass, not a wood, but when woven together, it is very strong. Bamboo grows quickly—stalks can grow 100 feet (30.5 m) in just six years. When harvested, the stalks are cut down, but the root system remains intact, allowing the bamboo to regrow quickly. For this reason, bamboo is generally considered a sustainable option.

Cork is another popular green option for flooring. Because cork comes only from the bark of a tree, it can be harvested without having to cut down the tree. The bark generally grows back in six to nine years, with no harm to the tree itself. Cork has the additional advantage of providing good insulation, protecting homes from both the summer heat and the winter cold.

Still, all choices have trade-offs. Some people say that bamboo is not as green as it appears to be. Most bamboo comes from China, and to meet the growing demand for bamboo, some Chinese companies are cutting down old-growth forests to make way for bamboo plantations. In addition, it requires significant energy to transport the bamboo from China all the way to the United States. Top-quality cork has the disadvantage of being hard to find and thus sometimes too expensive for the average homeowner to afford. As a result, many builders continue to rely on other, less sustainable wood products.

Shown here are samples of cork flooring.

When new wood is used, green builders make sure that it is taken from a certified sustainable forest. The Forest Stewardship Council (FSC), which was created in 1993, certifies forests that are managed to support the growth of new trees. The FSC label on furniture and other wood items ensures that these products are made from wood grown in forests that support sustainability principles.

Why Trees Are Necessary

Trees help the environment in many ways. For instance, they help clean the environment of toxic gases, even in urban areas, where there is much more concrete than there are trees. In New York City alone, there are about 5.2 million trees that help remove toxins from the air.

Trees also help shade homes and buildings, making them cooler and more energy efficient. The shade from trees also reduces people's exposure to harmful sun rays. Large pines and other evergreens are sometimes planted to block winter winds, reducing the amount of energy used for heating. Because leaves from trees keep rain from falling as quickly, trees also help reduce storm water runoff. Furthermore, trees provide a habitat for birds, squirrels, and many other animals that make up the ecosystem.

Some green builders also look for local materials. The closer building materials are to the site of the building, the less energy is required to transport them to the building site. Bill Grater, an architect in Clayton, New York, includes local materials whenever possible for his clients' houses. He used stones from an old quarry on Oak Island in Hammond, New York, for walls and fireplaces for two clients who built summer homes there. Using local materials not only makes environmental sense, it also makes sense artistically. Houses made from local stones and other building materials blend better with the surrounding landscape, which many people think makes the houses look nicer.

Recycled materials are another green choice. Items such as recycled rubber can be used to make flooring, and recycled

AFFORDABLE GREEN OPTIONS

"A lot of the high-profile green projects that get builders'
attention are very high-end, but the simple fact is that there
are plenty of strategies for inexpensive green building, from
right-sizing the structure to optimal value engineering to
reducing waste, among many others."

–Alex Wilson, founder of BuildingGreen, Inc.

Quoted in Rob Fanjoy, "Green Building Myths–Busted!," Louisville Home, Garden & Remodeling Show, accessed on May 31, 2019. www.louisvillehomeshow.com/Tips_and_Trends.aspx?id=55844350.

plastic has been used to build partitions between bathroom stalls in public buildings.

Reclaimed materials, which are taken from structures that have been torn down, are even better than recycled options. Wood, tiles, bricks, or stone can be taken from houses or other structures. "Whenever we can reuse a product instead of producing a new one from raw materials—even if those raw materials are recycled—we save on resource use and energy,"[20] explained the website Natural Building Solutions. Not only does using reclaimed materials save the cost of creating new ones, it also saves building materials from demolished sites from going to the landfill. In 2000, Alberici construction company, which is located in Overland, Missouri, decided to build its headquarters on a site that contained a three-story brick office building. Rather than demolishing the building and starting over, the company reused most of the materials from the building in its new facility, saving 97 percent of the materials from the landfill.

A building called the Ranch House in Del Sur, California, which received the highest LEED rating possible in 2007, also uses reclaimed materials. Rocks found at the site were used to build a chimney and fireplace, and planks from a demolished barn were used for the floors. Sunflower shells were ground up and made into cabinets. The Ranch House is insulated with cotton fibers and shredded scraps of blue jeans. The building can be reserved for conferences and events.

Some building materials are readily available and inexpensive. For example, some homes have been built of stacked wheat straw bales—a readily available agricultural product—covered with mud plaster so the house can withstand all different types of weather. According to Bob Brecha, the owner of one such home, his house uses only about 25 percent of the energy of a traditional house, making his heating bill only $100 per year. In contrast, heating bills for the average home in Dayton, Ohio, where Brecha's home is located, can cost between $800 and $1,000 per year. In addition to straw, some homes use recycled newspapers for insulation.

Manufacturers offer kitchen and bathroom countertops made from a variety of recycled materials, including recycled glass, paper, or aluminum. Homeowners have used the bottoms of wine bottles for glass partitions in their bathrooms or a back-splash for their kitchen sink. For a more rustic look, they might use branches stripped of their bark for porch railings.

Long-Term Energy Efficiency

When people think of conserving energy, they often think of turning off lights and other appliances when they are not in use. However, the process of conserving energy begins long before this point. Selecting the appropriate building materials in the first place can do far more to conserve energy than all of the things a person can do to try to save energy afterward. In fact, researchers indicate that state-of-the-art energy-efficient houses require only about 25 percent as much energy for heating and cooling as most existing houses. Although such houses can cost thousands more dollars to build, they save money on fuel and electricity expenses in the long run. For example, ENERGY STAR products use, on average, 10 to 50 percent less energy each year than other appliances.

Not all energy-efficiency measures require a lot of money. Improving energy efficiency begins by strengthening the protection from outdoor elements. This involves putting proper insulation in walls, ceilings, and floors. Well-insulated homes can save up to 30 percent on heating and cooling costs.

Urban Sprawl

Urban sprawl is the term given to a situation in which the population from crowded cities creeps further and further outward toward rural land. Commercial development begins, bringing urbanization to areas that used to contain only woodlands and forests. These changes in infrastructure not only cost taxpayers more money, they also increase traffic in rural and suburban areas. This, in turn, causes higher rates of air and water pollution. Development of concrete structures such as parking lots reduces the ability of the land to absorb rainwater, leading to a higher chance of flooding in homes.

Los Angeles, California, is a prime example of urban sprawl. Houses and large public buildings extend for miles outside the city center where the skyscrapers are.

High-efficiency windows with double-pane glass that do not let a lot of heat out of the house can further accomplish this goal.

Tinted windows, awnings, and carefully planted trees that take advantage of natural shade can make a house cooler in warm climates. Even paint color can make a difference. Houses in the southern part of the country tend to be lighter because lighter colors reflect more sunlight than darker ones, allowing the heat to bounce off the building instead of accumulating in it.

Green homeowners can also save energy by installing ceiling fans and thermostats that are set to heat or cool different rooms according to when they are in use. They may keep the water temperature on their water heater at a lower level and perhaps install a timer to efficiently heat the water when it is needed. Going green also involves making decisions about when and how to use appliances—running the dishwasher or washing machine only when it is full, for example. Some green consumers use monitoring systems to help them find out how much energy they are using and what they are using it for. At the Westcave Preserve Environmental Learning Center in Round Mountain, Texas, for instance, a monitoring system continually displays the amount of energy that is being used compared to what is generated from the solar panels on the roof.

Effective Use of Windows

Windows are important to energy-efficient buildings for several reasons. Windows that open to let in fresh air can save money on air conditioning, particularly if they allow cross-breezes from one side of the house to another. Well-placed windows can also help save energy otherwise needed for lighting a room. Daylighting is a technique used to maximize natural light so less electricity is needed to light the building during the day. In addition, because light bulbs generate more heat than light, daylighting can also save on the amount of energy needed to cool a space.

While many well-lit spaces include a lot of windows, experts emphasize that daylighting depends not on the number of windows but rather on where they are located, as well as how much light and heat they let into the building.

Committing to Carbon-Neutral Buildings

In 2018, the mayors of 19 cities around the world promised to enact policies to guarantee that all new buildings in their cities would be carbon neutral by the year 2030. This goal was part of the 2015 World Green Building Council held in Paris, France, where attendees focused on the need to curb the rise of global temperatures. To achieve this goal, builders will have to find ways to cut energy use in structures by up to 85 percent. According to Maureen Guttman, an architect at the Alliance to Save Energy, "Heating, cooling, hot water, and lighting are the primary loads in most buildings,"[1] accounting for around 40 to 50 percent of the total energy used around the world. Guttman said that building designers do not need to invent new technologies to cut energy usage, they just need to incorporate good insulation, ventilation, and other smart design choices in their structures. "Zero [carbon] buildings are being built without sophisticated materials or sophisticated equipment," Guttman said. "We have the technology."[2]

1. Quoted in Linda Poon, "What Will It Take to Make Buildings Carbon Neutral?," City Lab, September 12, 2018. www.citylab.com/environment/2018/09/what-will-it-take-to-make-buildings-carbon-neutral/569644/.

2. Quoted in Poon, "What Will It Take to Make Buildings Carbon Neutral?"

Daylighting strategies include using skylights, atriums, sloping ceilings, and other design features to eliminate dark corners. Researchers estimate that daylighting techniques used for the Lockheed Missiles & Space Company's office building in Sunnyvale, California, have reduced lighting energy use by about 75 percent compared to a conventional building.

Many public buildings also use motion detectors that automatically turn off the lights when people are not there. Green homeowners sometimes install motion detectors on their outside lights, automatically lighting up the pathway to the front door when needed. This saves people from having to keep lights on when they are out at night. People can also save electricity by installing dimmers that allow them to use less wattage when bright light is not needed.

The Abasto shopping mall in Buenos Aires, Argentina, is built in a way that maximizes natural light.

Energy On-Site

Some builders are using the power of wind or water directly on the site of a building. For example, the headquarters of the Alberici construction company won a LEED Platinum Award in 2004 for its use of solar panels to heat water and a 125-foot (38.1 m) tall wind turbine that provides the building with about 20 percent of its power. Wind currently provides only about 6 percent of America's total electricity, but by 2020, that figure is expected to rise to 15 percent or higher. Some people believe that wind may be a major source of energy in the future. Solar power is currently a more common source of electricity. Across America, solar panels placed on the roofs of buildings are helping provide power to homes, businesses, and even skyscrapers.

Actor Brad Pitt has said that he believes people can live comfortably without depending on fossil fuels. After Hurricane Katrina destroyed many houses in New Orleans, Louisiana, in 2005, Pitt founded a charity called Make It Right to build eco-housing for people who had lost their homes. Pitt stated that the energy-efficiency measures taken in building the homes would reduce upkeep costs by at least 75 percent. However, Make It Right ended up being a case study in the care that needs to be taken when designing and constructing buildings. In 2018, NBC News reported that many of the houses built by the charity had been abandoned because they were falling apart. The homeowners "complain of mold and collapsing structures, electrical fires and gas leaks. They say the houses were built too quickly, with low-quality materials, and that the designs didn't take into account New Orleans' humid, rainy climate."[21] The charity did not respond to these accusations or attempt to fix any of the homes, resulting in a lawsuit against Pitt and his organization. These issues show that, as with any building, the quality of both the materials and the construction play a large role in determining the effectiveness of an eco-friendly house.

In contrast to the Make It Right homes, a large amount of money and time was spent on One World Trade Center in New York City, making it one of the world's most energy-efficient skyscrapers. In 2016, it was designated the tallest LEED gold-certified building in the western hemisphere. Construction materials for One World Trade Center were made up of 40 percent recycled content. Normally, the building's all-glass exterior would lead to energy waste, but the glass materials are covered in a special coating that blocks out excessive heat from sunlight.

Solar panels are one way to make a house eco-friendly, but if the overall quality of the house is poor, the panels will not have enough of an effect.

Solar panels and other ways to capture alternative energy are unlikely to completely replace fossil fuels in most buildings—at least in the near future. One obstacle is that they are expensive. Still, the costs are coming down as more and more people are buying them. "Most of these [energy-efficient] technologies are becoming off-the-shelf now, and increasingly affordable," said Ashok Gupta, the NRDC's chief energy economist. "It's just a matter of convincing consumers to demand the technologies and educating developers to continue integrating them in a holistic way."[22]

In addition to the expense, alternative energy has other drawbacks. Water has been used as a source of power for many years; however, hydroelectric dams are not only expensive to build and maintain, but they also require swiftly running water. Solar panels only work where—and when—the sun shines, and significant space is required to install the number of panels needed to provide energy for a large building. Similarly, wind power is generally not an option in mountainous or forested areas where the wind is blocked. Even in windy areas, such as the Great Plains, wind farms require a lot of physical space to produce electricity. Therefore, in areas where there is not a lot of available land, they are not a good option for providing energy.

Conserving Water

Many green buildings go beyond traditional energy savings to look for ways to conserve water as well. Like other resources, water is limited. Although 70 percent of the earth's surface is covered by water, less than 1 percent of this water can be used by humans. Some of the unusable water is polluted, too salty, or trapped under ice, so saving the usable water is important.

Green homeowners can fit their showers and faucets with fixtures designed to conserve water. The EPA mandates that showerheads use no more than 2.5 gallons (9.5 L) of water per minute, and some water-saving showerheads that use much less water have become common. Toilets that flush a lot or a little water depending on how much is needed can conserve up to 80 percent of the annual water usage of a typical toilet. In some places where water is especially scarce, people have installed sinks on top of their toilet tanks. Because the water that refills the toilet is clean, it is suitable for people to wash their hands with. The water then fills up the toilet tank.

Some buildings have green roofs—literally. They have grass, plants, and sometimes even trees on their roofs. These green roofs help absorb rainwater and keep it from pouring off the building and washing soil away. In urban settings, they also create some green space for people and animals to enjoy.

Green walls are an option too. More and more frequently, designers are adding plants into the designs of their buildings. For instance, two buildings in Milan, Italy, called Bosco Verticale, or "vertical forest" in Italian, have plants covering the outside walls. The variety of different plants "create[s] a microclimate that produces moisture, absorbs carbon dioxide, produces oxygen as well as providing protection against radiation and pollution."[23] Although the buildings are in the middle of a city, they provide the same benefits as up to 215,278 square feet (20,000 sq m) of forest.

Shown here is one of the two Bosco Verticale buildings in Milan, Italy.

Landscaping Alternatives

Landscaping involves how the yard around a building is designed and the kinds of plants and trees that are used. Using gravel driveways or stone pathways rather than paved surfaces is one way landscapers are going green. Paved surfaces are impermeable, which means they do not allow water to seep back into the ground. Impermeable surfaces increase both the amount of water that runs into streets and gutters and the speed at which the water leaves the land. Runoff is not good for plants. It also picks up pesticides and fertilizers that are used to treat lawns and carries them into waterways. Some people believe that pesticides and fertilizers are responsible for 10 percent of the nation's water pollution.

There are many unique landscaping options that are more sustainable than a lawn.

Green advocates suggest cutting back on the amount of lawn used in landscaping, particularly if maintaining a beautiful grassy lawn requires a lot of chemicals and mowing. Cultivated turf in the form of the grass lawns grown around homes, golf courses, and public parks might be considered the largest irrigated "crop" in the United States. Covering around 40 million acres of land, grass takes up more space than cotton, livestock pastureland, wheat, and hay combined. Each year, Americans use more than 17 million gallons (64 million L) of fuel to power gas lawnmowers and other equipment used to maintain their lawns. Chemical runoff from fertilizers that are used to keep lawns healthy has become a major source of pollution. Water from hoses and sprinkler systems accounts for between 30 and 60 percent of urban water usage.

Some landscapers are covering the ground around homes and in parks with ivy or other groundcovers that sprawl across the ground but do not grow tall. These eliminate the need for mowing and use far less water than grass. Homeowners can choose to landscape with more trees and shrubs or to create pathways and patios out of gravel, which allows rainwater to seep back into the ground. Alternative choices for groundcover vary by location, as homeowners need to account for the climate of their region and must select vegetation that naturally grows there, since introducing plants from other parts of the country can disturb the natural habitat of an area.

Grassy sports stadiums require huge amounts of water and fertilizer to maintain, so they are not very eco-friendly.

CHAPTER 4

Buying Green

According to the Organic Trade Association, the growth rate for sales of organic food items outpaced the growth of the overall food market by 600 percent in 2017. This shows that people are starting to take more of an interest in where their food comes from and how it is grown. However, it is not just organic foods that Americans are interested in: Sales of organic non-food products hit a record-breaking $4.2 billion in 2017 as well. Today, people are increasingly willing to spend more money buying products they believe are better for their bodies, their families, and the planet. With products such as green deodorants, shampoos, laundry detergents, and kitchen cleaners, Americans are looking for alternatives to the potentially toxic chemicals found in conventional products. What is on the outside counts too, as more and more people look to purchase products that are packaged in sustainable materials, thereby decreasing the use of disposable plastics. A growing number of consumers are trying to protect the earth by making green choices in the products they shop for.

Eating Organic

Organic foods are grown without insecticides, fertilizers, or other pollutants that can end up in the land or waterways. Some people buy organic foods because they have less impact on the earth than other produce; many people also believe that these foods taste better and are healthier. While taste is a personal matter, several studies have found that organic foods have little to no increased health benefits compared to non-organic foods.

To purchase organic food, people used to have to go to farm stands or farmers' markets where farmers bring their crops, or join a food cooperative that buys food from local organic farmers. Over the past several decades, however, supermarkets specializing in organic foods have sprung up in communities across America. Whole Foods is the biggest of these chains. As a growing number of consumers began to search out organic foods, major supermarket chains also began carrying organic produce as well as natural foods. According to the Mayo Clinic, the terms "organic" and "natural" are not interchangeable, although they are frequently used that way. On a food label, natural "means that it has no artificial colors, flavors or preservatives. It does not refer to the methods or materials used to produce the food ingredients."[24]

Growing organic food requires more time and attention. Without artificial fertilizers, plants may not grow as big or produce as many fruits or vegetables. Without pesticides, some crops may also be lost to bugs or other pests. In addition, organic foods are not treated with preservatives, so they may not be able to be transported as far or last as long. The lower yield—the amount that can be sold—means that the farmer will have to sell the produce at a higher price to make money. As a result, organic foods tend to cost more than other foods.

An increasing number of Americans are willing to pay higher prices for organics. From 1997 to 2017, sales of organic food grew from $3.4 billion to $49.4 billion. Some parents, such as

ORGANICS: NOT BETTER, NOT WORSE

"Organic agriculture is just another method of agriculture–not better, not worse. This is like any other merchandising scheme we have, which is providing customers what they want. For those customers looking for an organic alternative in things like Rice Krispies, we now have an alternative for them."

–Bruce Peterson, head of perishable food at Wal-Mart

Quoted in Melanie Warner, "Wal-Mart Eyes Organic Foods," *New York Times*, May 12, 2006. www.nytimes.com/2006/05/12/business/12organic.html.

a woman named Kim Dennis, believe that the satisfaction of choosing a healthier alternative is worth the price. Dennis noted, "If [my children] eat a whole pint of berries, that's a lot of pesticides for their little bodies."[25]

Closely related to the organic movement is the desire for fruits, vegetables, and other foods that are grown locally. Green consumers generally believe that buying local foods is better for the environment. Food that is grown nearby is frequently fresher because it gets to the store or farm stand faster. Buying locally also means that food is not transported great distances, decreasing fuel consumption and air pollution. Furthermore, many people enjoy supporting local businesses rather than large corporations. Buying locally produced food gives these small farms the resources they need to keep growing their food organically.

Eco-Friendly Personal Care

Consumers are fueling a growing demand for organic and sustainably produced health and beauty products. According to the Organic Trade Association, Americans spent $350 million on organic personal products in 2006—$68 million more than in 2005. This trend has continued since then, and the website Market Watch reported in 2018 that the worldwide natural and organic personal care market is expected to expand to $29.5 billion by 2028. Companies that exclusively market natural products, such as Burt's Bees, Jason Natural Cosmetics, and Tom's of Maine, are experiencing rapid growth in sales, and other companies that do not sell organic products have cashed in on the trend by introducing special organic lines. For example, in 2019, the website MindBodyGreen published an article reviewing several natural beauty products that were available at Sephora. Several organic companies, including Origins and Nature's Gate, have received certification for some of their products from the U.S. Department of Agriculture (USDA) proving that their products contain organic ingredients.

In addition to using organic ingredients, many companies are also experimenting with better ways to package their products. Rather than wrapping something in layers of plastic that will end up in a landfill, some products are now packaged in biodegradable boxes—or no packaging at all. For example, in an effort to eliminate plastic toothpaste tubes, a company called Bite has created what it calls "toothpaste bits." These small, pill-shaped bits come in a glass bottle; the user bites down on them to activate them, making them foam up like any other toothpaste. Lush Cosmetics also offers its own brand of toothpaste tablets. Another packageless product Lush offers that has been gaining popularity is shampoo bars. These bars look like soap but contain shampoo ingredients. Since they are solid rather than liquid, there is no need for a plastic shampoo bottle.

Experts caution that natural products may not always be as healthy as people assume, however. "Consumers should not necessarily assume that an 'organic' or 'natural' ingredient or product would possess greater inherent [natural] safety than another chemically identical version of the same ingredient," cautioned Linda M. Katz, the director of the FDA's Office of Cosmetics and Colors. "In fact, 'natural' ingredients may be harder to preserve against microbial contamination and growth than synthetic raw materials."[26]

Jane Houlihan, the vice president of research for the non-profit Environmental Working Group in Washington, D.C., agreed. In their effort to attract green consumers, Houlihan said, some companies are using new natural products that have not been properly tested for safety. "Just because an ingredient comes from a plant does not necessarily make it safe to use in a cosmetic," Houlihan explained. "Tobacco, hemlock and poison ivy are all examples of plants that can be hazardous."[27]

Some consumers are so fed up with the thought of not being able to trust what is good and what is bad in their products that they resort to making their own. Ingredients such as glycerin

Some products, such as soap, are easy to make at home in a more eco-friendly way than large companies do.

and shea butter are in almost all bath products, and they are inexpensive to purchase as raw materials. From there, it is easy for people to add additional ingredients, such as scented oils, to customize their own soaps.

Sustainable Clothing

Although people are most familiar with organic foods, other materials are organic as well. Clothing, sheets, and upholstery for chairs and sofas can be made from cotton, wool, silk, or hemp that has not been treated with chemicals or pesticides.

Patagonia was considered a pioneer when it switched to organic cotton in 1996. "Going organic was a difficult decision for us," said a spokesperson for the company. "Ethically it made perfect sense, but it was expensive and hard to come by. Today, thanks to our friends and customers, we're still selling organic cotton clothing, and more and more businesses are making the switch because you voted with your dollars."[28]

The website Quartz noted that there are other concerns people need to think about when trying to buy the most environmentally friendly cotton clothing, such as what kinds of dyes were used; non-organic dyes create a lot of waste water and use a lot of chemicals, and it is almost impossible for someone to figure out whether or not the dyes used in their clothing were organic. Quartz offered this advice to people who want to have as little negative impact as possible on the environment:

> Buy better clothes. Buy less of them. Wear them more. There's no more certain way to reduce your impact than to reduce the amount of clothes you consume and to keep those clothes for a long time. Just try to wash them only as needed. Laundry uses a lot of water and energy, too.[29]

Today, Patagonia and many other retailers are looking for more alternative sustainable options. Hemp has become a popular fiber with both consumers and manufacturers. It is a sustainable choice for fiber because the hemp plant is quick and inexpensive to grow, using as little as half the amount of water required to cultivate cotton. The lightweight fabric woven from it is durable and versatile.

Like bamboo, the hemp plant can be used to make many items, such as rope and cloth.

The bamboo plant can also be processed and woven into fiber used to make clothing. Bamboo requires little water and no fertilizers to grow at an astonishingly fast rate. However, converting this tough, woody material into clothing fiber requires an intensive chemical process that may not be as sustainable as hemp or other fibers.

Green Cleaning

Using green cleaning products is another way people can reduce the impact their home makes on the environment. There are a number of "eco-cleaners" on the market that work as well as conventional cleaning fluids. They do not give off harmful fumes or pollute the water supply when washed down the drain.

Green consumers can also clean their homes with cleaners they make at home out of natural ingredients such as water, vinegar, and baking soda. By purchasing empty plastic bottles and refilling them each time they make more cleaning solution, consumers can also cut down on the amount of plastic packaging they use. However, just because these cleaners are natural does not mean they are not dangerous if they come into contact with the skin or eyes, or if they are accidentally ingested. Even with eco-friendly products, consumers should also be careful not to mix ingredients that can give off harmful fumes when combined.

Too Much Plastic

The amount of plastic packaging used to display and ship goods is overwhelming. Some people say that plastic is society's greatest garbage challenge. According to the EPA, packaging amounts to more than one-third of a city's solid waste by weight. According to the website EcoWatch, the average American discards about 185 pounds (84 kg) of plastic per year, making the total for the United States alone roughly 65 billion pounds (29 billion kg). Used for everything from toys to automobile parts to food containers, plastics never biodegrade. Over hundreds of years, plastic may break down into smaller particles, but it releases toxic gases in the process. In addition to the energy needed to dispose of or recycle the plastic after it is used, it takes a great deal of energy to make the plastic in the first place.

Green manufacturers and designers are searching for solutions through groups such as the Sustainable Packaging Coalition. In the meantime, many people are looking for opportunities to reduce their dependence on plastics, especially single-use plastics such as bags and water bottles. One of the easiest ways to do this is for people to bring their own reusable bags when they go shopping, but there are other things consumers can do as well. When they buy fruits and vegetables, they may put them right into the grocery cart rather than the plastic bags supermarkets provide, or bring their own cloth bags. They may also look for nuts, beans, and other goods that can be bought in bulk instead of coming pre-packaged in plastic.

SENDING A MESSAGE

"What I hear as I talk to people is this phenomenal sense of despair about their inability to do anything about climate change, or the disparity [gap] between rich and poor. But when they go into a grocery store they can do something—they can make decisions about what they are buying and send a very clear message."
–Marion Nestle, a nutritionist at New York University and the author of *Food Politics*

Quoted in "Voting with Your Trolley," *Economist*, December 7, 2006. www.economist.com/business/displaystory.cfm?story_id=8380592.

Beth Terry, a woman who runs a blog called *My Plastic-Free Life*, documents her efforts to use as little plastic as she possibly can. For example, she uses glass bottles to hold her bulk foods and sends back packaging to online retailers with a letter urging the company to reconsider its use—or overuse—of packaging. "In my efforts to tread lightly on the earth, I am seeking to reduce the amount of waste I produce considerably," she wrote in one post. "I find extra packaging ... to be unnecessary, and ... [plastic] is not biodegradable and will last in the environment forever, whether it is recycled or not."[30]

However, not everyone can make this kind of commitment. So many things come in plastic that it can be very difficult, time-consuming, and expensive to avoid it. While many non-plastic items are usable for longer, which makes them cheaper in the long run because they do not have to be replaced as often, they generally cost more up front. For someone who does not have a lot of money to spend, some eco-friendly items may be out of their price range. Furthermore, even if people can afford to spend more on certain products, many people dislike the idea of paying more for the things they already get cheaply. However, this attitude seems to be changing. In a 2002 survey by *Packaging World* magazine, 61 percent of respondents said they would not be willing to pay more for green packaging. In contrast, a 2015 survey by Nielsen found that 66 percent of consumers would pay more for sustainable items. Millennials, or people born between 1981 and 1996, were especially likely to give this answer.

Plastic or Paper?

Plastic bags have become the focus of a huge debate in recent years. They are one of the most commonly used single-use plastics. Many people do not recycle them; they simply throw them away. This can be a problem because the bags are so light that they sometimes blow out of garbage cans and end up as litter.

Although plastic bags can be recycled, many cities do not accept them in recycling bins. Some large stores do accept plastic bags for recycling, but many people do not like to make a special trip to drop them off and find it more convenient to throw them away. Others may not realize their city does not accept plastic bags for recycling and throw them in their recycling bin anyway. When mixed in with other recyclable items, single-use plastic bags can cause trouble. They fill with water and dirt and get caught in sorting machinery at recycling plants, where they slow down the process and end up in the trash anyway. Like all plastic, the bags will never biodegrade.

A lot of plastic waste ends up on the beach and in the ocean, posing a danger to marine life. Animals such as sea turtles often mistake plastic bags for jellyfish and eat them, which can kill or sicken them. Birds can get caught in plastic bags and have difficulty flying, which also makes it difficult or impossible for them to find food.

The Great Straw Debate

Plastic straws have become the subject of fierce debate in recent years. They do not make up the biggest portion of plastic waste, but they are small and easily overlooked. They are rarely recycled, and when they are, they are so lightweight that sorting machines often miss them, which means they contaminate loads of non-plastic recyclables. Straws make up 4 percent of all the trash that ends up in the ocean, where they can do a lot of harm to wildlife. For all of these reasons, many places have started banning plastic straws, giving them out only when people ask for them, or replacing them with paper straws. In 2018, for instance, Seattle, Washington, banned plastic straws throughout the city.

As plastic straws have come under fire, more companies have begun selling straws made out of other materials, such as metal or bamboo. These need to be washed after being used instead of thrown away, so many restaurants do not offer them; instead, people who want to use non-plastic straws generally buy one and carry it around with them, washing it themselves after they use it. Some people applaud these moves and have made an effort not to use plastic straws at restaurants. Others think giving up straws is such a small step that it will make no difference.

One often-overlooked group of people—those with motor disabilities—has found severe problems with the straw ban. For some people, straws are an essential tool to help them drink. National Public Radio (NPR) explained,

> There are many alternatives to plastic straws … But paper straws and similar biodegradable options often fall apart too quickly or are easy for people with limited jaw control to bite through. Silicone straws are often not flexible—one of the most important features for people with mobility challenges. Reusable straws need to be washed, which not all people with disabilities can do easily. And metal straws, which conduct heat and cold in addition to being hard and inflexible, can pose a safety risk.[1]

Many people with disabilities, as well as their caretakers and loved ones, want straw bans to be less limiting. Many people—both with and without a disability—believe that someone who does not need a straw should refuse to take a plastic one or buy a reusable one but that plastic straws should be available for those who truly need them.

1. Tove Danovich and Maria Godoy, "Why People with Disabilities Want Bans on Plastic Straws to Be More Flexible," NPR, July 11, 2018. www.npr.org/sections/thesalt/2018/07/11/627773979/why-people-with-disabilities-want-bans-on-plastic-straws-to-be-more-flexible.

In recent years, U.S. cities and states have begun initiatives to tax or outlaw single-use plastic bags. In March 2008, San Francisco, California, became the first U.S. city to outlaw the use of plastic grocery bags. The entire state of California followed suit in 2018, and every county in the state of Hawai'i has voted to ban the bags. In 2019, New York State lawmakers also began plans to ban stores from providing consumers with plastic bags by 2020. According to New York governor Andrew Cuomo, "these bags have blighted our environment and clogged our waterways." He noted that the plan would help "protect our natural resources for future generations of New Yorkers."[31]

Some people think paper bags are better than plastic because they are easier to reuse and are biodegradable. However, paper bags also have disadvantages. They are thicker than plastic bags, so they cost more to transport. In addition, the process of making paper bags uses up much more water and at least as much energy as the process of making plastic bags. Furthermore, like plastic bags, most paper bags end up in landfills after one use. Paper does not degrade in landfills as well as most people think. This is why the greenest solution is for people to bring their own reusable bags when shopping.

IS ORGANIC FOOD REALLY GREEN?

"You cannot say that all organic food is better for the environment than all food grown conventionally. If you look carefully at the amount of energy required to produce these foods you get a complicated picture. In some cases, the carbon footprint for organics is larger."

—Ken Green, professor of environmental management at Manchester Business School, England

Quoted in Cahal Milmo, "Organic Farming 'No Better for the Environment,'" *Independent*, February 19, 2007. environmentalnews.blogspot.com/2009/02/organic-farming-no-better-for.html.

Reducing Packaging

Bottled water is emerging as another hot topic. A 2007 article by Charles Fishman in *Fast Company* magazine reported that North

Americans spent $15 billion on bottled water in 2006. By 2017, according to data from the Beverage Marketing Corporation, that number had risen to $18.5 billion. The process of making plastic requires oil; Fishman stated that making plastic bottles uses the same amount of oil as 100,000 cars each year. Most of these bottles—85 to 90 percent of them—are thrown out, mostly because people tend to use them when they are on the go.

Talk show host Ellen DeGeneres counts not recycling plastic water bottles among her pet peeves. She said,

> I've seen people drinking water out of plastic bottles and then not recycling them. That's infuriating. I know it's faster to throw it in the garbage. But if you're going to buy water individually bottled for your convenience, then all I say is, take the time and put it in the can marked "Recycle." It's a small thing that makes a big difference.[32]

Plastic water bottles produce a huge amount of waste. To try to cut down on some of it, many public places have installed water bottle filling stations to make it easier for people to carry a refillable water bottle with them.

Some green consumers say that it does not make enough of a difference to recycle these bottles. They say that people should not use the bottles in the first place. Not only is energy wasted in the process of bottling water, they say, but it also wastes water. Buying a filter for the kitchen tap and filling a heavy-duty reusable bottle with tap water is a far greener strategy.

In some places, though, bottled water is a necessity because the available water is not clean enough to drink. In many developing countries, water must be boiled or filtered before it can be drunk. This makes staying hydrated on the go difficult unless someone buys bottled water. The water in most of the United States is generally safe to drink, although some people do not like the taste of tap water and prefer to use filters. One exception is the town of Flint, Michigan, where old water pipes have broken down and released toxic chemicals such as lead into the water. Many people have criticized the state and federal government for being slow to repair these pipes. As a result of this issue, people in Flint have no choice but to drink bottled water, as even boiling or filtering will not make their water safe to drink or even bathe in.

The strategy of eliminating packaging can be extended to any individually packaged item, not just water bottles. Rather than purchasing juice boxes for school lunches, for instance, green consumers might buy a large container of juice and pour it into a reusable bottle. The same goes for individually packaged snack foods: Buying crackers, cookies, and chips in large packages and putting them into reusable containers for school can reduce waste considerably.

Of course, not all packaging is automatically bad, even if it is not recyclable. Some packaging protects goods and keeps them from getting broken or damaged during transport. In this way, packaging reduces waste by preventing the broken items from being thrown out. Packaging may also maximize the amount of a product that can be packed into a larger container. As a result, fewer containers—and thus fewer trucks—may be needed to move the same amount of goods. This means fewer greenhouse gas emissions in the end.

Reuse and Recycle

Another option for green shoppers is buying items that have been used by someone else. Sometimes people sell things after only one use. When people buy used computer games, videos, building blocks, or books, they are saving the raw materials and energy needed to make new ones.

Buying used clothing at a thrift store can help cut down on the amount of energy that goes into creating new clothes. It also prevents old clothes from ending up in a landfill.

Green consumers also look for products with recycled content, such as napkins, toilet paper, plastic bottles, and other items. Products can contain anywhere from 5 percent to 100 percent recycled material. For example, the Love Beauty & Planet line of personal care products, such as shampoo and hand soap, comes in 100 percent recycled bottles.

Many green consumers say recycled products are indistinguishable from conventionally produced ones. One reporter set out to compare paper products made with recycled content to those made with new paper. While his family was away, he replaced his household's paper products with recycled brands. "After three days and zero comments, I took that as a sign that we could live happily ever after with recycled,"[33] he reported.

It used to be difficult to find green products, but an increasing number of companies recognize that going green is good for business. In an effort to attract green consumers, retailers are adding products made from organic, recycled, and recyclable materials. For example, Wal-Mart introduced its own line of organic products in 2006. With more retailers offering more options, green products are not only becoming easier to find, they are becoming less expensive as well. Many people have already shown that they are willing to pay a bit more for products that are better for the environment. Many more will likely go green as costs become more competitive.

CHAPTER 5

Reducing Humanity's Impact on the Earth

In the 1980s, residents living near the beach in Brittany, France, began to notice something strange. Each year, hundreds of plastic novelty phones washed up on their 15-mile (24 km) stretch of beach. The phones, modeled after the popular cartoon cat Garfield, littered the beach with orange plastic, virtually intact despite the decades they had spent in the ocean. In 2019, the source of the phones was finally discovered: A lost shipping container was found trapped in a sea cave, accessible only at low tide.

The eyeless faces of the orange cat and the receivers of the phones are collected by the hundreds by environmental organizations, including Ar Viltansou, a local beach clean-up group. According to the group's president, Claire Simonin Le Meur, a complete clean up and excavation of the lost shipping container is impossible. However, an unintended use has emerged for these phones: They are found with such frequency and are so easy to spot that they are now used as an indicator to track the movement of plastic in the ocean.

This story teaches an important lesson about plastic: Once it gets into the environment, it is there to stay. "I cannot imagine that these phones could ever be completely destroyed, given their state of conservation after more than 30 years in the water," said Le Meur. "The oceans do not 'digest' plastic; sometimes it transforms it into microplastics, which are even more dangerous for fauna and flora."[34]

For more than 30 years, Garfield phones such as this one have been washing up on a beach in France.

According to the EPA, U.S. residents, businesses, and institutions produced more than 262 million tons of waste in 2015—about 4.6 pounds per person per day. The amount of trash the average American throws out is at least twice as much as the amount thrown out by the average person in western

Europe. Most of this trash is disposed of in landfills, but a lot of trash never makes it that far. Lightweight plastics such as grocery bags, straws, six-pack rings, and product packaging blow out of trash cans and into streets, forests, and waterways.

Floating in the Pacific Ocean halfway between California and Hawai'i is an island of trash, collected there by ocean currents. This island, known as the Great Pacific Garbage Patch, covers more than 600,000 square miles (1,553,993 sq km) of ocean—an area twice the size of Texas. According to researchers, the trash comes from all over the world and weighs about 88,000 tons. It contains materials such as abandoned fishing nets that trap animals such as seabirds, fish, seals, and dolphins. Sometimes the animals become caught in the garbage and die, unable to escape. Other times, they swallow pieces of trash that get caught around their mouths or in their digestive tracts. Every day, the planet's wildlife is more and more threatened by the trash produced by humans.

To combat this problem, educators emphasize the "three Rs" of going green—reduce, reuse, and recycle. Reducing begins with the consumer. In addition to conserving energy and water, reducing includes thinking about the choices someone makes when shopping. Avoiding packaging, buying used products, and buying only what is needed are the main strategies for reducing waste.

Recycling Goods

Recycling materials is different than reusing them. Recycling converts old products into new ones by mechanical or chemical methods. Used steel or aluminum cans, for instance, can be shredded, melted, and then reformed to make new cans or other products.

In decades past, most Americans thought little about throwing everything into the trash. The few people who thought to recycle had to take their recyclables to one or more collection centers. These recycling centers, which were generally located on the outskirts of town, were hard to find, had limited hours, and required people to sort their recyclables by material. Although these measures helped the centers reduce costs—and therefore made recycling economically feasible—it made recycling inconvenient for individuals. Today, recycling is easier and more accessible. According to the EPA, the recycling rate has increased from just 7 percent in 1960 to 35 percent in 2018.

Donating for Others

Rather than throwing out things they no longer want, green consumers look for places to make donations. Some charity organizations have special drop-off centers; others pick up items from a person's home, making going green easier than ever.

Habitat for Humanity, a nonprofit organization that helps build homes for low-income families, accepts tools, building materials, furniture, and appliances in good working order. The organization sells these items in their ReStores to help raise funds. Thrift stores such as Goodwill operate local centers that accept household and clothing items for resale.

Specialty stores often accept specific donations. Office Depot and Staples, for instance, accept toner cartridges and some other types of office supplies so they can be properly recycled instead of thrown away. Clothing brands such as H&M and Converse also run recycling programs; people can drop off old clothes and shoes at these stores–even ones that are not in good condition–so they can be recycled, saving the product from ending up in a landfill. Eyeglass stores often collect eyeglasses for the needy. Local charity organizations, hospitals, libraries, schools, day care centers, homeless shelters, and churches are also often in need of household goods, clothing, books, and toys.

To encourage people to comply with recycling rules, some local governments provide bins for sorting recyclables and carrying them to the curb. In addition to paper, cans, and plastic, some local governments hold special collection times for yard waste, Christmas trees, and used appliances. Waste Management, one of the nation's largest trash companies, states that up to 25 percent of all items in recycling bins are actually trash. The company urges people to reduce this amount by recycling clean, empty bottles, cans, paper, and cardboard, as well as keeping foods, liquid, and plastic bags out of the recycling bin.

As computers have become more widespread, the idea of "going paperless" has also grown. In the past, people would receive all their bills through the mail; today, many businesses offer incentives to get people to sign up for bills, invoices, and bank statements that are delivered electronically. However, even with this move, paper still accounts for a large amount of waste.

Many offices still rely on paper documents. These create a lot of waste when they are no longer needed.

The process of making new paper from old is relatively simple and uses just half of the energy required to make new paper from trees. Making entirely new paper "is one of the most environmentally harmful industries on earth," wrote Elizabeth Royte in her book *Garbage Land*. "It depletes the forests and their biodiversity, it uses more water than any other industrial process in the nation ... and it dumps billions of gallons of water contaminated with chlorinated dioxin and a host of other hazardous and conventional pollutants into rivers, lakes, and harbors."[35]

One of the difficulties with paper recycling is that prices do not stay steady. In 1993, the average selling price of recycled paper was $46 per ton; just two years later, the price had jumped to $165 per ton. In the first decade of the 21st century, the price went back to $50 per ton. Because buyers cannot know how much they will have to pay for recycled materials from one year to the next, such extreme price changes make it difficult for buyers to be able to plan. This forced some early recycling programs to shut down.

Even so, Allen Hershkowitz of the NRDC emphasized the importance of recycling paper at any cost. "We've got to keep doing it, even if we're just holding the line," he said. "Conservatively, timber harvests would expand fifty percent in the next thirty-five years if we didn't recycle paper."[36] If people want to have continued access to paper, as well as to trees, paper recycling is not optional.

Plastic, Metal, and Glass Materials

Most metal is dug out of the ground through mining—a process that is harmful to the environment. Digging into the land damages habitats, destroys natural resources, and produces carbon dioxide and acid rain. Finding and extracting metals also requires a substantial amount of energy.

Fortunately, metals are relatively easy and cost effective to recycle. Working with clean recycled steel instead of creating new steel from raw materials also cuts air pollution by more than 85 percent and water usage by 40 percent. Furthermore, recycling steel conserves enough energy annually to power about 18 million homes for a full year. According to the Steel Recycling Institute, 70 million tons of steel scrap is recycled each year—enough steel to build 189 professional football stadiums.

American households can do their part by recycling cans. According to the Aluminum Association, a group made up of aluminum producers and recyclers, aluminum is the most valuable recyclable, yet Americans throw more than $700 million worth of aluminum cans in the garbage each year. Recycling

Easy Ways to Go Green

Everyone can go a little more green. Below are just a few easy lifestyle changes people can make.

- Walk or bike to nearby places.
- Carry reusable silverware, a stainless steel straw, and a bottle or cup for eating and drinking on the go.
- Carpool to school events and parties, or offer a neighbor a ride.
- Take shorter showers. Turn off the water when it is not in use.
- Use rechargeable batteries in games and other electronics.
- Use less electricity by turning off the television, radio, and lights when no one is in the room. Unplug clocks, radios, and other appliances before going on vacation.
- Avoid plastic baggies and individually packaged items.
- Instead of covering leftovers in plastic wrap, choose glass containers with reusable lids or an eco-friendly option such as Bee's Wrap (cloth covered in beeswax).
- Look for ways to make things last longer, such as using both sides of paper when printing things on the computer. Donate things that are no longer wanted or needed.
- Re-wear clothing that is not dirty. Hang dry clothing instead of putting it in the dryer; this uses less energy and makes clothing last longer.
- Recycle newspapers, glass, plastic bottles, and aluminum cans. Rinse them out and sort them according to the requirements of the collection agency.
- Buy products made from recycled materials.
- Compost biodegradable materials, such as food scraps, instead of throwing them out.
- Organize a local trash clean up.

aluminum takes a fraction of the energy needed to make new aluminum; in fact, recycling just one can saves enough energy to listen to a full music album on an iPod. Because aluminum can be recycled over and over again without losing its strength or durability, nearly 75 percent of all the aluminum that has ever been produced is still being used today and can continue to be used in the future if people recycle it instead of throwing it out.

Similarly, glass can be recycled over and over again without losing its quality. One exception is glass that has been treated to withstand very high temperatures, such as oven-safe cooking dishes. After glass jars and bottles are electronically sorted according to color, they are generally ground down by machines and then made into new bottles. Recycling glass requires less energy than recycling plastic or aluminum. It also saves as much as 95 percent in raw materials. However, as with cans, many people find it more convenient to throw glass into the trash. Furthermore, even though glass is more environmentally friendly, glass packaging is harder to find because glass containers are heavier and therefore more expensive to ship, so manufacturers are increasingly replacing glass jars with plastic.

Because there are so many different kinds of plastics, it is more expensive and time-consuming to recycle. Containers first must be sorted by type. In most cases, the type of plastic used for a container is identified with a numbered triangle symbol on the bottom. Most city recycling programs accept only some kinds of plastics.

Recycling plastic involves crushing the sorted containers into small pieces that are then melted or treated with chemicals. The resulting liquid plastic is formed into

Not all plastic is recyclable, so the items that end up at the recycling plant need to be sorted. Shown here are several men sorting through plastic bottles at a recycling center in Mumbai, India.

new products. In addition to new plastic containers or parts, re-cycled plastic is sometimes woven into fiber that is used to make carpets or clothing. Fabrics such as nylon, fleece, faux (fake) leather, and elastics are made from plastic. These materials are widely used in clothing because they are inexpensive and versa-tile. However, these articles of clothing are often cheaply made, and consumers have found that they generally do not last more than one season. Clothing that is not donated, reused, or given to a fabric recycling program ends up in landfills.

Many people do not like to spend a lot of money on clothing, but clothing that is inexpensive is generally cheaply made, so it wears out more quickly. More expensive clothing tends to last longer, so people spend less money on clothes in the long run. However, price is not always an indication of quality: Even expensive clothing is sometimes made with cheap plastics that do not last and are soon thrown away.

Manufacturers also re-form used plastic into outdoor furni-ture, decks, and docks, replacing the wood once used for these purposes. The plastic goods cost more than wood, but many consumers say they are worth the extra cost. Because they will not be damaged by being outdoors in all kinds of weather or be eaten by bugs such as termites, the plastic items will last much longer.

Marketing Recycled Goods

The last step of the recycling process for any material is selling the new product. Unfortunately, it can be hard to find markets for some types of recyclables. Many companies generally prefer new plastic, for instance, because it is of more consistent quality than recycled plastic. The new plastic is guaranteed to be free of incompatible materials that are sometimes mixed in when the plastic is not sorted well before recycling. Manufacturers say it is also easier to control the color of plastics that have no recycled content. Similarly, paper manufacturers complain that recycled paper often gets dirty during collection and sorting. The added expense of cleaning the paper makes it too expensive to use for some purposes.

A THROW-AWAY SOCIETY

"We live in a throw-away society. You'd be amazed at what some people throw away—everything from bathtubs to books. But the truth is, there's no such place as 'away.'"

–David Bach, environmentalist

David Bach and Hillary Rosner, *Go Green, Live Rich: 50 Simple Ways to Save the Earth and Get Rich Trying.* New York, NY: Broadway Books, 2008, p. 88.

Some companies believe that putting "recycled" on the label will make people think that the quality of the item is poor. "Consumers have long been trained to think of previously used stuff as inferior," explained Richard C. Porter, an economist and author of *The Economics of Waste.* "This training goes back centuries, to the time when recycled clothing made of recycled rags was called 'shoddy,' and the very word 'recycled' became a synonym for second rate."[37] Although recycling has come a long way thanks to improved technology, many people still think of recycled materials as worse than new ones. Many people also prefer to simply throw something in the trash and forget about it rather than spend time making sure the items in their recycling bin are clean and able to be recycled.

Is Recycling Effective?

Some people say that recycling is a waste of time and money. At a public hearing in March 2006, Tom Phillips, an elected official in Greensboro, North Carolina, claimed,

> *The net cost for recycling is more than double the cost for regular garbage collection that will go to the transfer station. (This is after selling the recyclables we can.) A lot of what we recycle winds up at the landfill anyway because of contamination or lack of markets for the recycled material … While [recycling] "feels good" it is too expensive and we must look for better alternatives.*[38]

Some economists argue that recycling will occur naturally when there is a market for recyclables, as with large pieces of scrap steel and aluminum. Michael Munger, a political science professor at Duke University, believes that recycling makes no sense for other items. "There is a simple test for determining whether something is a resource (something valuable) or just garbage," Munger wrote. "If someone will pay you for the item, it's a resource … But if you have to pay someone to take the item away … then the item is garbage."[39]

The fact that there needs to be a market for recyclables is something most people do not think about. Someone has to be willing to buy the materials and put the effort into transforming them. Up until 2018, China was importing two-thirds of the world's plastic waste, but this ended up causing social, economic, and environmental problems for the country. For this reason, it put new rules into place that restricted what could be sent to China, meaning the United States now has to work on improving its own recycling programs. According to the *Week*, "America's recyclable waste is piling up in landfills. But even before China started refusing shipments, our recycling system failed to actually recycle more than a fraction of the waste that went into it. Simply put, America's recycling system isn't efficient enough to deal with the amount of stuff Americans consume."[40] In the United States, recycling is generally "handled by private companies that partner with local governments … Profits depend on how expensive it is to just make new commodities with new materials."[41] Without the incentive of money, many places choose not to recycle. For this reason, some people have proposed taxing landfills to make it more expensive to throw things out than to recycle. Others have suggested new regulations that would prevent companies from using the types of materials that are harder to recycle. Additionally, technology is still advancing. For instance, new machines that are better at sorting materials into the right piles can help make the process more efficient.

In some cases, the process of recycling some products creates more pollution than it is worth. Recycling simply may not be the answer for many of the materials that are currently commonly used. Ann Leonard, an expert in international sustainability and environmental health issues, explained, "True closed-loop recycling has no new resource input and no waste output. And that's virtually impossible with plastic waste because its chemical structure changes when it's heated and the quality degrades. We're just delaying its eventual dumping."[42]

Natural Composting

Composting is generally done at home rather than being organized by large companies. It can be a very effective way to recycle food scraps, yard waste, and other organic materials and keep them out of landfills.

A compost bin (shown here) is a good way to put organic waste to use. When it fully decomposes, the compost can be used to help a garden grow.

The EPA indicates that 24 percent of the U.S. waste stream is made up of yard trimmings and food scraps. Composting is a system that turns these items into mulch, which has nutrients in it that can feed a garden. Airflow is one important part of composting; a compost pile must be turned frequently to allow the air to get to all the materials in the pile and help them decompose.

Many websites have information for families who are interested in starting a compost pile, and a number of products—such as bins to house the compost and boxes to help aerate it—are readily available. Generally, composting consists mainly of separating out fruit and vegetable peels, coffee grounds, yard waste, and other organic materials, putting them in a backyard compost bin or heap, and turning the pile to aerate it. Nature does most of the rest of the work.

Some companies and schools also compost the waste from their cafeterias. Brentwood Elementary School in Brentwood, Texas, for instance, collects several pounds of leftover raw fruits and vegetables from the cafeteria each day to add to its compost pile. The school's gardening and environmental clubs maintain the compost piles and use the finished compost in the school gardens.

Not everyone has a yard where they can compost their organic waste. One option for people who live in apartments is worm compost, also called vermicompost. This type of composting is increasing in popularity among green advocates in urban areas, and some have found that the worms turn material into usable compost in as little as 60 days. According to Joan D. Filsinger, an avid gardener who wrote about her vermicompost, "There's little or no odor, and no heavy lifting. And, best of all, my worms make compost in a compact container right in my own home."[43]

Local governments have also begun to establish central composting sites. Most often, these composting sites are used mainly for yard waste such as dead leaves and twigs, but some also allow some types of food scraps to be included. In many cases, after the material has been composted, the city gives or sells the compost back to citizens, who use it in their yards or gardens. In this way, government composting programs provide two services: They keep organic waste out of landfills, and they provide compost material at reasonable prices.

The number of cities that provide composting services for residents has increased exponentially. Across the nation, the number of municipal composting sites rose from 651 in 1989 to 4,713 in 2017. State governments have also passed laws designed to reduce the amount of yard waste. Thirty-five states recycle yard trimmings, food scraps, or wood, and twenty-one states have banned these materials from landfills.

Like most green practices, composting has its critics. Tom Outerbridge, who works with a nonprofit called City Green in New York City, said, "People think composting is the greatest system in the world. But it takes a lot of energy to make it work—to deal with odor abatement and collecting it and turning it to aerate it."[44] Outerbridge noted that when cities offer compost pickup, this puts more trucks on the road. "Those trucks have a huge environmental impact," he said. "And then there are all the trucks and bulldozers pushing the compost around at the facility."[45]

There are also other expenses involved in composting on a large scale. Most yard waste is collected in the summer and fall, then made into mulch, which is then sold in the spring. Space is needed to store it, which can be expensive in urban areas. It can also be difficult to find buyers.

Still, advocates point out that the benefits of composting far outweigh the drawbacks. In a 2009 publication, the University of California Division of Agriculture and Natural Resources wrote,

Composting is good for several reasons:

- *It saves water by helping the soil hold moisture and reduce water runoff.*
- *It benefits the environment by recycling organic resources while conserving landfill space.*
- *It reduces the need for commercial soil conditioners and fertilizers.*

Compost provides many benefits. It

- *adds nutrients and beneficial microbes, holds water, and improves plant growth*
- *provides a supplemental amount of slow-release nutrients*
- *increases soil organic matter*
- *encourages healthy root structure*
- *lightens clay soils and helps sandy soils hold water*
- *attracts and feeds earthworms and other beneficial soil microorganisms*
- *helps balance pH (acidity/alkalinity)*
- *helps control soil erosion*
- *helps protect plants from drought and freezes*
- *decreases use of petrochemical fertilizers*
- *moderates soil temperature and reduces weeds when used as mulch*[46]

The Future of the Earth

No matter what people do, they will make an impact on the earth. It is impossible for an organized society to offer food, shelter, transportation, and other necessities to such a large population without having any effects at all on the environment. The goal is to find the options that will make that impact as small as possible.

As the human population grows, the only thing that can save the planet is a global acknowledgement of the impact of human activity on the environment and a global effort to reduce that impact. So far, most lawmakers have failed to make the kind of drastic changes needed to reverse the effects of climate change and pollution on the earth. Now it is up to the leaders of tomorrow to make their voices heard and push for environmental initiatives in their communities.

Around the world, kids and teens are demanding action from the adults who control the laws governing environmental practices. From student walkouts and demonstrations to writing books that plead for change, young people all over the world are showing that they care about the future of the planet. At the 2017 climate change summit in Bonn, Germany, 12-year-old environmental activist Timoci Naulusala called for the "global village" to recognize the impact of climate change. "Ladies and gentleman, speeches and talks won't solve the problem," he said, "but to walk the talk is more effective."[47]

Naulusala is right. For today's youth, climate change is an inevitable part of the future. However, if people are aware of the issues and take matters into their own hands, they might make the changes that will make a difference.

Chapter 1: Why Americans Are Going Green

1. "Climate Change 2014 Synthesis Report: Summary for Policymakers," Intergovernmental Panel on Climate Change, 2014, p. 2. www.ipcc.ch/site/assets/uploads/2018/02/AR5_SYR_FINAL_SPM.pdf.

2. "Climate Change 2014," Intergovernmental Panel on Climate Change, p. 4.

3. Quoted in Roger Ebert, "An Inconvenient Truth Movie Review (2006)," RogerEbert.com, June 1, 2006. www.rogerebert.com/reviews/an-inconvenient-truth-2006.

4. Quoted in "An Inconvenient Truth for Al Gore," Confederate Yankee, March 13, 2007. confederateyankee.mu.nu/archives/218760.php.

5. Quoted in Jesse Ellison, "Testing the Validity of Eco-Claims," *Newsweek*, June 28, 2008. www.newsweek.com/testing-validity-eco-claims-91149.

6. Quoted in "The Six Sins of Greenwashing—Misleading Claims Found in Many Products," Environmental News Network, December 3, 2007. www.enn.com/articles/26388.

Chapter 2: Traveling Green

7. Tanya Mead, "Why I Walk 2 Miles to the Store Instead of Driving," Alternative Daily, accessed on May 3, 2019. www.thealternativedaily.com/benefits-of-walking/.

8. Quoted in Larry Copeland, "Healthy Alternative: Take Mass Transit," *USA Today*, January 31, 2008. www.usatoday.com/news/nation/2008-01-31-masstransit_N.htm.

9. "Metro News Release," Washington Metropolitan Area Transit Authority, April 21, 2008. www.wmata.com/about/news/pressreleasedetail.cfm?ReleaseID=2067.

10. Quoted in Kevin Kantola, "Yellow Taxis Going Green with Propane," Hydrogen Cars Now, March 18, 2008. www.hydrogencarsnow.com/blog2/index.php/competition/yellow-taxis-going-green-with-propane.

11. Tom Mutchler, "Not Always Keen Going Green: Honda Civic GX," Consumer Reports, February 14, 2008. www.consumerreports.org/cro/news/2008/02/not-always-keen-going-green-honda-civic-gx/index.htm.

12. Elizabeth Rogers and Thomas M. Kostigen, *The Green Book: The Everyday Guide to Saving the Planet One Simple Step at a Time*. New York, NY: Three Rivers Press, 2007, p. 86.

13. Sophie Uliano, *Gorgeously Green: 8 Simple Steps to an Eco-Friendly Life*. New York, NY: HarperCollins, 2008, p. 251.

14. Uliano, *Gorgeously Green*, p. 251.

15. Quoted in Ellison, "Testing the Validity of Eco-Claims."

Chapter 3: Greener Homes

16. "Earthship Design Principles," Earthship Biotecture, accessed on May 3, 2019. www.earthshipglobal.com/design-principles.

17. Quoted in "Eco-Friendly Buildings," PBS, April 15, 2005. www.pbs.org/newshour/show/eco-friendly-buildings.

18. Quoted in "Eco-Friendly Buildings," PBS.

19. Quoted in Matt Woolsey, "Nine Earth-Friendly Fixes for Your Home," *Forbes*, April 14, 2008. www.forbes.com/2008/04/14/green-home-energy-forbeslife-cx_mw_0414realestate.html.

20. Alex Wilson, "What Makes a Product Green," Natural Building Solutions, last updated February 1, 2006. getnaturalusa.com/makes-product-green/.

21. Brandy Zadrozny, Kit Ramgopal, and Farnoush Amiri, "Brad Pitt Built Dozens of Homes in New Orleans After Katrina. Now They're Falling Apart and Residents Are Suing," NBC, September 12, 2018. www.nbcnews.com/news/us-news/brad-pitt-built-dozens-homes-new-orleans-after-katrina-now-n908651.

22. Quoted in David Bach and Hillary Rosner, *Go Green, Live Rich: 50 Simple Ways to Save the Earth and Get Rich Trying*. New York, NY: Broadway Books, 2008, p. 38.

23. "Five Plant-Covered Buildings for a Greener Environment," *Jakarta Post*, September 3, 2018. www.thejakartapost.com/life/2018/09/02/five-plant-covered-buildings-for-greener-environment.html.

Chapter 4: Buying Green

24. "Organic Foods: Are They Safer? More Nutritious?," Mayo Clinic, April 4, 2018. www.mayoclinic.org/healthy-lifestyle/nutrition-and-healthy-eating/in-depth/organic-food/art-20043880.

25. Quoted in Carole Marie Cropper, "Does It Pay to Buy Organic?," *Bloomberg Businessweek*, September 6, 2004. www.bloomberg.com/news/articles/2004-09-05/does-it-pay-to-buy-organic.

26. Quoted in Natasha Singer, "Natural, Organic Beauty," *New York Times*, November 1, 2007. www.nytimes. com/2007/11/01/fashion/01skin.html.

27. Quoted in Singer, "Natural, Organic Beauty."

28. Quoted in Kara DiCamillo, "Patagonia Celebrates 10 Organic Years," TreeHugger, October 4, 2006. www.treehugger. com/sustainable-fashion/patagonia-celebrates-10-organic-years.html.

29. Marc Bain, "Your Organic Cotton T-shirt Might Be Worse for the Environment Than Regular Cotton," Quartz, May 28, 2017. qz.com/990178/your-organic-cotton-t-shirt-might-be-worse-for-the-environment-than-regular-cotton/.

30. Beth Terry, "Dear (Blue Vinyl DVD Distributor) New Video," *My Plastic-Free Life*, May 13, 2008. myplasticfreelife. com/2008/05/dear-blue-vinyl-dvd-distributor-new/.

31. Quoted in Jesse McKinley, "Plastic Bags to Be Banned in New York; Second Statewide Ban, After California," *New York Times*, March 28, 2019. www.nytimes.com/2019/03/28/nyregion/plastic-bag-ban-.html.

32. Quoted in Rogers and Kostigen, *The Green Book*, p. 13.

33. Miguel Llanos, "Ready to Rethink Toilet Paper for Earth Day?," NBC News, April 21, 2006. www.nbcnews.com/id/12318915/ns/us_news-environment/t/ready-rethink-toilet-paper-earth-day/.

Chapter 5: Reducing Humanity's Impact on the Earth

34. Quoted in Connor Boyd, "The Beach Where Hundreds of Garfield Phones Wash Up Every Year: Novelty Items from

the 1980s Pollute French Shore—and Demonstrate the Dangers of Plastic Pollution," MSN, February 26, 2019. www.msn.com/en-us/news/world/the-beach-where-hundreds-of-garfield-phones-wash-up-every-year-novelty-items-from-the-1980s-pollute-french-shore-and-demonstrate-the-dangers-of-plastic-pollution/ar-BBU62O3#page=2.

35. Elizabeth Royte, *Garbage Land: On the Secret Trail of Trash.* New York, NY: Little, Brown, 2005, p. 136.

36. Quoted in Royte, *Garbage Land*, p. 137.

37. Richard C. Porter, *The Economics of Waste*. Washington, D.C: RFF Press, 2002, p. 12.

38. Quoted in Michael Munger, "Think Globally, Act Irrationally: Recycling," Library of Economics and Liberty, accessed on May 31, 2019. econlib.org/library/Columns/y2007/Mungerrecycling.html.

39. Munger, "Think Globally."

40. Jeff Spross, "America Has a Recycling Problem. Here's How to Solve It," *Week*, February 11, 2019. theweek.com/articles/819488/america-recycling-problem-heres-how-solve.

41. Spross, "America Has a Recycling Problem."

42. Quoted in Royte, *Garbage Land*, p. 189.

43. Joan D. Filsinger, "Worm Composting: Wriggling Recyclers Transform Kitchen Scraps into Compost," *Fine Gardening*, accessed on May 31, 2019. www.finegardening.com/article/worm-composting.

44. Quoted in Royte, *Garbage Land*, p. 115.

45. Quoted in Royte, *Garbage Land*, p. 114.

46. Pamela M. Geisel and Donna C. Seaver, "Composting Is Good for Your Garden and the Environment," University of California Division of Agriculture and Natural Resources, September 2009. anrcatalog.ucanr.edu/pdf/8367.pdf.

47. Quoted in Loic Tchinda, "5 Young Environmental Activists Making a Difference in Climate Change," UN CC:Learn, June 21, 2018. medium.com/uncclearn/5-young-environmental-activists-making-a-difference-in-climate-change-f211e070ab53.

DISCUSSION QUESTIONS

Chapter 1: Why Americans Are Going Green

1. Explain some reasons other than going green why people might buy hybrid cars or energy-saving appliances.

2. How have local governments and businesses made it easier to go green?

3. What do you think is the most important reason for going green?

Chapter 2: Traveling Green

1. Do you think biofuels can ever completely replace fossil fuels? Why or why not?

2. Would you rather have a hybrid or an electric car? Explain your answer.

3. What is one downside to walking or riding a bike instead of driving or taking public transport?

Chapter 3: Greener Homes

1. What factors should green builders consider when selecting building materials?

2. Would you want to live in an Earthship? Why or why not?

3. What are some alternatives homeowners can choose instead of planting grass for their lawns?

Chapter 4: Buying Green

1. Do you think organic materials are worth the extra cost? Why or why not?

2. Are organic or natural products always better for you? Explain your answer.

3. What are some ways you can go green with your personal care products?

Chapter 5: Reducing Humanity's Impact on the Earth

1. How is reusing something different than recycling it?

2. What are some things you can change to make your lifestyle greener?

3. List five items you think can be composted and five items you think cannot be.

ORGANIZATIONS TO CONTACT

Action For Nature
2269 Chestnut Street, #263
San Francisco, CA 94123
www.actionfornature.org
www.instagram.com/actionfornature
twitter.com/ActionForNature

> Action For Nature is a U.S.-based nonprofit organization that inspires young people to take action for the environment and protect the natural world, both in their own neighborhood and globally.

Alliance to Save Energy
1850 M Street NW, Suite 610
Washington, DC 20036
www.ase.org
twitter.com/ToSaveEnergy
www.youtube.com/user/AllianceToSaveEnergy

> The Alliance to Save Energy promotes energy efficiency worldwide to achieve a healthier economy, a cleaner environment, and greater energy security.

Earthship Biotecture
2 Earthship Way
Tres Piedras, NM 87577
www.earthshipglobal.com
www.instagram.com/earthship
twitter.com/earthship_HQ

> Earthship Biotecture is educating individuals on the design principles of building structures out of natural and reclaimed materials such as old tires and recycled cans and bottles. The organization also provides relief efforts to areas that need it after natural disasters.

National Environmental Education Foundation (NEEF)
4301 Connecticut Avenue NW, Suite 160
Washington, D.C. 20008
www.neefusa.org
www.instagram.com/neefusa_org
twitter.com/neefusa
www.youtube.com/user/NEEFusa/featured
> NEEF was created in 1990 to advance environmental knowledge
> and action with the ultimate goal of promoting environmentally
> responsible behavior in the general public.

U.S. Department of Energy
1000 Independence Avenue SW
Washington, D.C. 20585
www.doe.gov
www.instagram.com/energy
twitter.com/energy
www.youtube.com/user/USdepartmentofenergy
> The U.S. Department of Energy provides information about
> energy efficiency and alternative sources of energy.

FOR MORE INFORMATION

Books

Bailey, Loren. *30-Minute Sustainable Science Projects.* Minneapolis, MN: Lerner Publications, 2019.
> Part of going green is reusing things instead of throwing them out. The projects in this book use everyday objects to teach people about science.

Centore, Michael. *Environment & Sustainability.* Broomall, PA: Mason Crest, 2017.
> The author explores how communities and individuals are taking part in the green movement and being more mindful of sustainability.

Snedden, Robert. *Environmental Engineering and the Science of Sustainability.* St. Catharines, ON, Canada: Crabtree Publishing, 2014.
> Learn how engineers create products that are both easy to use and good for the environment.

Spilsbury, Louise. *Environment at Risk: The Effects of Pollution.* Chicago, IL: Raintree, 2006.
> This book focuses on how people and pollution affect the earth. It discusses many key environmental issues facing the planet today, including global warming, acid rain, air and water pollution, and the overuse of nonrenewable resources.

Wilcox, Charlotte. *Recycling.* Minneapolis, MN: Lerner, 2007.
> This book focuses on the science of recycling and explains the many amazing ways people use science to turn garbage into great things.

Websites

Blue and Green Tomorrow

blueandgreentomorrow.com

> This website provides trending news on eco-tourism, the energy industry, and ways to become more energy efficient at home.

Environmental Literacy Council

www.enviroliteracy.org

> The Environmental Literacy Council is dedicated to helping students understand environmental issues. Its comprehensive website contains resources on almost every aspect of the natural world.

EPA: Recycle City

www.epa.gov/recyclecity

> This interactive website includes information and games that help teach people about reducing, reusing, and recycling.

EPA: Student Center

www.epa.gov/students

> This website, hosted by the U.S. Environmental Protection Agency, offers activities and resources for teachers and students of all ages, including information on environmental basics, recycling, and conservation.

Student Conservation Association

www.thesca.org

> This website provides resources to foster the next generation of conservation leaders, placing students in internship positions in national parks across the country.

INDEX

PICTURE CREDITS

ABOUT THE AUTHOR

Juliana Burkhart is a native of Buffalo, NY, currently living in New York City. She teaches and performs acrobatics and hand balancing with a local circus troupe. She is a writer, artist, and dog lover who enjoys spending time outdoors hiking and camping.